RECOVERY FROM ALCOHOLISM

RECOVERY FROM
• ALCOHOLISM •

A Social Treatment Model

ROBERT G. O'BRIANT, M.D.
Director of Alcoholic Services
San Joaquin Medical Facilities

HENRY L. LENNARD, Ph.D.
Professor of Medical Sociology (Psychiatry)
University of California, San Francisco

and

Steven D. Allen, Ph.D.
Lecturer, Division of Ambulatory & Community Medicine
University of California, San Francisco

Donald C. Ransom, Ph.D.
Assistant Professor of Ambulatory and Community Medicine
University of California, San Francisco

With a Foreword by:

MARTY MANN
Founder-Consultant
National Council on Alcoholism

CHARLES C THOMAS · PUBLISHER
Springfield · Illinois · U.S.A.

Published and Distributed Throughout the World by
CHARLES C THOMAS · PUBLISHER
BANNERSTONE HOUSE
301-327 East Lawrence Avenue, Springfield, Illinois, U.S.A.

© *1973, by* CHARLES C THOMAS ● PUBLISHER
ISBN 0-398-02830-3
Library of Congress Catalog Card Number: 73-194

With THOMAS BOOKS *careful attention is given to all details of manufacturing and design. It is the Publisher's desire to present books that are satisfactory as to their physical qualities and artistic possibilities and appropriate for their particular use.* THOMAS BOOKS *will be true to those laws of quality that assure a good name and good will.*

Printed in the United States of America
H-1

This book is dedicated to Thorsten "Benny" Benton

1909-1969

FOREWORD

This is an exciting book about an exciting project, and in my opinion everyone working in this field, as well as everyone interested in alcoholism and the treatment of alcoholics, should feel compelled to read it.

The subtitle "A Social Treatment Model" gives only the faintest clue to the scope and breadth of the imaginative, innovative treatment program, which in essence is demonstrating a startingly new attack on the most difficult and, in the past, non-rewarding area of this problem. It could be called a heart-warming example of man's humanity to man. From the underlying philsophy on through every component of the program, far more than ordinary concern for the patient is shown. Understanding, sympathy and full recognition of the alcoholic's human dignity built a solid base for a well thought out plan to meet his needs.

Starting with the assumption that *rehabilitation* implies restoring someone to a *habilitated* past, the architects of this program recognized that most of their patients had no such past to which they could be returned. Stockton has a high rate of alcoholism within a high rate of unemployment: migrant workers make up much of this group, and many of them are chronic court offenders. If they were to have a chance of recovery, not just they, but their environment had to be treated, and over a period of time. This could be a prohibitively costly effort. The San Joaquin County program found ways to accomplish this with a comparatively reasonable outlay of funds, largely because they staffed their project with a minimum of highly-paid professionals, and large numbers of counselors who are recovered alcoholics.

There are four components to this environmental approach: 1) a detoxification unit, 2) an inpatient unit, 3) a medical unit for medical problems only, and 4) a Social Center used by all patients over an open-ended period, with men housed in an annex and the women in the Center itself.

Many evidences of what is really happening here show through in the book. For instance, the detoxification unit is staffed by non-professionals whose major treatment is their constant presence and their deep caring. As a result, there have so far not been cases of DT's, rarely convulsions, and this despite the absence of medications.

For literally thousands of years, man has known of the beneficial effects of love. Here in San Joaquin its therapeutic value is being demonstrated. And the program is therefore attracting many patients from a wider range of economic and social levels than the original group for whom it was devised. Truly, love works for all men.

MARTY MANN
Founder-Consultant
National Council on Alcoholism

INTRODUCTION

O<small>NE OF THE</small> most misunderstood conditions of man is also one of the leading health problems in the United States today. Alcoholism must be ranked among the three most serious national health problems, together with heart disease and cancer.

We suspect that if all the facts were available, alcoholism would have to be considered the most widespread and costly health problem in the country. Estimates of the number of alcoholics in the United States range upward from 9,000,000. Such estimates are difficult to verify because alcoholism is a hidden health problem, concealed because of the social stigma attached to it. Yet it has been pointed out again and again that persons suffering from alcoholism and alcohol related medical problems place a considerable strain on clinic and hospital facilities, and the social costs for the alcoholic, his family, and the community are virtually incalculable.

Death certificates and medical records fail to reflect the extent of alcoholism as the primary or even secondary cause of death. The death certificates of individuals committing suicide or those dying from overdoses of various medications frequently do not mention alcoholism even when it is a major or contributing factor. For example, of 1,400 alcoholics who participated in our inpatient treatment program at Bret Harte Hospital, fifty are known to have died after returning to drinking subsequent to their hospitalization. We discovered that in only three cases was alcoholism listed on the death certificates as either cause or contributing factor. All of the fifty had been diagnosed as confirmed alcoholics, and yet this lethal problem was not noted on forty-seven of the death certificates.

Every physician who sees adult patients in his practice encounters many alcoholics. It is not uncommon, however, even for physicians to ignore or fail to perceive this fact. Many patients exhibit physical and psychological complications of alcohol abuse. In most cases, discussion of alcohol use is avoided by both the physician and the patient when exploring the patient's symptoms. Physicians often feel uncomfortable inquiring about the use of alcohol, and many alcoholics tend to deny, avoid, or lie about their alcohol use. This leads to frustration and misunderstanding on the part of the physician and adds to the frustration, confusion and hopelessness of the alcoholic.

The social and psychological consequences for the alcoholic and for those who must live and work with him are considerable. The alcoholic himself sooner or later faces incalculable losses in social functioning and human dignity. His parents, spouse, or children either tolerate him, despite the unhappiness and turmoil he creates, or reject him. His exclusion from the family inevitably generates bitterness and guilt.

Disappointment and frustration are also great for those who treat the alcoholic. Hospital and clinic staffs and physicians in private practice soon recognize that the alcoholic will return repeatedly for help with the same or more severe alcohol related problems. The regular reappearance of the alcoholic in the emergency room or the private office strains the patience and resources of our medical delivery systems.

Alcohol must be classified as a *potent psychoactive drug.* Its effects are harmful, even devastating, to millions of persons. Alcohol also is an addictive drug. Yet, in today's society an individual who does not drink is considered strange or deviant. Alcohol consumption is part of daily life, but we are at a loss to deal with its effects. We know that alcohol is harmful but fail to understand and provide for those who have become addicted to this *legal, socially acceptable chemical.*

Alcoholism is a condition that carries a social stigma, and in that sense would have to be grouped with leprosy, tuberculosis, epilepsy and venereal disease. The stigma is all the more severe because the majority of Americans use alcohol without difficulty while demonstrating very little tolerance or understanding for those who cannot use it without becoming addicted.

Until recently problems generated by alcohol use, whatever their severity, were seen to be the result of a derelict will or a disturbed mind. Once in the medical system, the alcoholic was usually labeled a mental problem. The treatment of alcoholism has been viewed as within the province of psychiatry. The significant effect of this historical accident is that a specific treatment for the alcoholic has not been devised within the medical system. Alcoholics have been treated as criminals by the legal system and as mentally disordered by the medical system, but rarely as alcoholics, with any differentiated and special attention being paid to the alcoholic syndrome itself. The treatment modalities employed were, with some exceptions,* those available for other psychological disturbances.

It is significant that the major exception to this trend is represented by Alcoholics Anonymous, an organization designed specifically for the alcoholic and his problems and one which developed independent and apart from the medical-mental health system. Free of the implicit assumptions and models of the health professions, Alcoholics Anonymous has been sensitive to the peculiar predicament and needs of the alcoholic and developed its own "theory" of alcoholism and methods to arrest its course in an addicted individual.

Aside from the work of Alcoholics Anonymous, the alcoholic has been subject to a set of erroneous assumptions which grow out of a mechanistic model of human behavior and behavior change, a *man as machine* model. The treatment of alcoholism is seen as a technological challenge. In this model, alcoholism is a disease in which something has gone wrong with the "physical hardware." The task is to repair the physical structures of the organism or supply a drug to rebalance the human machine.

But little, if anything, is known about what has gone wrong with the "hardware" and there is no drug specific to arrest the course of alcoholism. As a result, the alcoholic is being "treated" with each new chemical remedy that becomes available. The same holds true for psychodynamic and behavioral approaches. Whatever form of treatment is in vogue for the mentally disturbed or behaviorally disordered is applied to the alcoholic. From psychonanalysis to marathon encounter groups, from insulin coma and electroshock to aversion therapy, everything that has been used with the mental patient has been tried on the alcoholic.

---

* Among the exceptions is the use of chemical substances (Antabuse) which were designed to deter alcohol use. Of course, some individual alcoholics have been helped by almost every one of the modalities employed (psychotherapy, group therapy, aversive conditioning, etc.) although these *treatments* were not specifically designed for them.

The alcoholic often is the victim of the same errors committed with a wide range of *problematic people* who become the province of professionals specializing in changing persons. The helping agent applies the available "treatment" rather than applying himself to the problem at hand. Only too often he perpetuates the status quo or makes things worse rather than being genuinely helpful. Available treatments generally derive from an implicit model describing the nature of man and a formula for change. When the basic model is in error or when the treatments are not relevant to the problem the person on the receiving end is ill served.* This has been the plight of the alcoholic.

Yet there is ample evidence that many alcoholics do recover. There are many hundreds of thousands of sober, recovered alcoholics living in this country, but they are invisible as a group. Many have become anonymous, not primarily as a result of the philosophy and tradition of Alcoholics Anonymous, but because of the stigma attached to alcoholism. They are anonymous in a society that misunderstands and rejects them. They are anonymous because they have been designated as a special group of persons considered unemployable and thought to have neglected their families, their health and their social obligations. Yet many sober alcoholics are functioning and accomplishing those things society has condemned them for neglecting.

The recovery rate from alcoholism may well be far better than from most chronic diseases, the difference being that the recovered alcoholic in most cases does not need or use professional follow-up to verify his recovery. Many professionals and agencies, however, view alcoholism as an irreversible and malignant process since they deal only with those alcoholics who continue to drink and therefore fail to recognize that many individuals stop drinking, recover, and live normal and productive lives. It is becoming increasingly clear that the addictive processes of alcoholism promise to be controlled most effectively within a social model, a model that sustains sobriety, in which the alcoholic learns to live without the further use of this drug. The purpose of this book is to explain this model of social reconstruction and to describe a program which is based upon it.

---

* When treatment is ineffective, the client is generaly considered responsible. He is then described as poorly motivated, or is given a diagnosis such as *borderline psychosis, inadequate personality,* or some other perjorative designation.

ACKNOWLEDGMENTS

SAN JOAQUIN COUNTY, California, as most communities in this country today, faced the difficult task of providing care for alcoholics. We recognized that present treatment models for accomplishing this task were inadequate and outdated. The revolving door system (jail, hospital, welfare, courts) that exists in most communities only perpetuates the problem. Alcoholics are hospitalized on a haphazard basis and then dismissed to return to their drinking environment, in many cases to the skid row area of the community. This treatment arrangement is damaging to the morale of those who deal with the alcoholic, and, of course, it does not provide the alcoholic with the opportunity for rehabilitation.

Dr. Louis M. Barber, Administrator of the San Joaquin County Medical Facilities, realized the inadequacies of current approaches to the alcoholic individual and was dissatisfied with the care provided. Under his direction planning was begun in the summer of 1969 to provide a comprehensive treatment program for alcoholic individuals residing in this county. In 1969 Dr. Barber presented to San Joaquin Board of Supervisors a plan to extricate the alcoholic from the revolving door system and place him in an on-going program where recovery might be possible. The Board of Supervisors adopted the plan; all have wholeheartedly supported its realization. Dr. Barber and the San Joaquin Board of Supervisors have shown vision and courage in sponsoring a program that departs significantly from conventional methods of treatment.

Thorsten "Benny" Benton, to whom this book is dedicated, foresaw the need for a social treatment program to assist in the recovery of alcoholics. The program also could not have been developed without the tireless cooperation and devotion of a group of counselors, all of them, sober alcoholics. We are in their debt!

Finally, for a careful reading of the manuscript, and many thoughtful suggestions we thank Mrs. Florette White Pomeroy, of the National Council on Alcoholism; Dr. Leon J. Epstein of the University of California, and Dr. Allen J. Enelow of the Pacific Medical Center.

CONTENTS

RECOVERY FROM ALCOHOLISM

Chapter I

CURRENT APPROACHES
TO TREATMENT

A discussion of current models of treatment of the alcoholic, their basic similarities and why they have been relatively ineffective.

IT IS A widely held belief that alcoholism is a problem of the individual and that he is to blame for his misfortune. In the common sense view of the problem, alcoholism is a matter of will power and of character. The public believes the alcoholic to be deficient in these qualities, and sees him as a victim of his own failings and therefore not worthy of sympathy or action in his behalf.

The professional view of the alcoholic has, until recently, not been very different: Alcoholism is seen as a problem of the individual. Psychoanalysts see the alcoholic, like other addicts, as suffering from an aberrant psychological make-up. Physicians with an organic orientation see alcoholism as the result of the individual's faulty biochemical make-up.

Models of Treatment

In most professional treatment programs, the alcoholic is subject to the erroneous premise that alcoholism is wholly a disease of the individual, either psychological, physiological, or some combination of both. Acceptance of this basic premise leads to treatment efforts aimed at producing some change within the individual, such that he may, after some limited period of time, be discharged from treatment as cured, and henceforth will have no problems with alcohol.

Virtually all alcoholism treatment programs are alike in their ad-

[3]

herence to this individual disease oriented model. The *differences* between programs are the result of different assumptions regarding the individual's disease and the appropriate strategy for producing change in the individual. The dichotomy in treatment programs is between those which concentrate on physiological strategies, including *chemotherapy* and those which stress *psychotherapeutic* operations. The distinction between the two types of major treatment efforts current today is a small one, and both are limited in scope and in comprehension of the problem.

Models underlying treatment require continuous reexamination. Medical care is organized around models of illness and treatment. Each model involves conceptions of illness, of etiology, and definitions of the unit of illness and treatment. Each model delineates the boundaries of medical responsibility and concern. For example, the responsibility of a physician who diagnoses and treats a typhoid fever patient does not cease when he has rendered medical care to his patient. In this instance, his responsibility includes a search for the source of the infection and the protection of those who are in danger of being infected by the patient. Or let us consider the physician's responsibility to the patient who has diabetes. Competent medical care here would include a thorough explanation of the disease, including a discussion of hereditary implications, the dangers of infection, circulatory problems, cataracts, as well as instruction to the patient regarding what he must do to control the disease: use of insulin, urine analysis, diet, exercise, etc. In other words, the physician must help the patient to understand his illness and to change the patterns of his everyday behavior which interfere with its control. He must remain an active force in the life of his patient until he is assured that the patient's way of life has changed in ways which will reduce the dangers from the disease.

When models of illness and treatment are inappropriate or incomplete, serious consequences may ensue. Efforts based on such models may be ineffective, and a great many resources, both personal and financial, are expended without significant outcome. This creates pessimism within treatment agencies, funding institutions, and the general public, regarding the possibility of successful treatment.

In extreme instances, treatment based on the wrong model results in *fall out* more lethal than would have occurred had no medical intervention been used. An example of such consequences of the wrong model is where the patient's condition is misdiagnosed and procedures are commenced (surgery, potent medication) which endanger the health of the individual.

Most alcoholism programs, whether privately supported or sponsored by city, county, state, or federal government, do not adequately understand the disease of alcoholism, the units of illness and treatment, and the extent of medical responsibility to the alcoholic. Considerable effort and resources of many hospitals, especially of state, city, county, and V.A. hospitals and clinics, are expended in the treatment of serious alcohol related medical problems (delirium tremens, withdrawal symptoms, liver failure, gastric hemorrhage). While heroic treatment efforts are often life saving in the short run, they have little effect in changing the long range patterns of the patient's alcohol use. He is most often discharged without learning about the nature of his illness and with no plans for follow-up treatment. Many of those receiving treatment re-enter the community only to return weeks or months later with the same or more severe medical problems created by the use of alcohol. This state of affairs exacts a heavy toll in the morale of medical and nursing personnel who work with alcoholic patients, often knowing fully well that the result of their labors will be short lived. Nonetheless, in terms of the model of illness and treatment within which they operate, they are powerless to change this vicious cycle.

Private physicians also tend to treat only the physical symptoms in terms of this same, short term medical model. They usually refrain from making the diagnosis of alcoholism, due both to shortage of time and to their wish not to stigmatize the patient. They may, however, prescribe tranquilizing and sedating drugs for such patients. Rather than alleviating the alcohol problem, this kind of medical treatment only leads to the creation of a dual problem, a dependence on psychoactive drugs added to the dependence on alcohol.*

Some state hospitals and private alcoholism hospitals move beyond

---

* Many alcoholics report that their initial exposure to sedatives and tranquilizers, on which they came to depend for relief of symptoms associated with alcoholism, was through their physicians. About 40 percent of those alcoholics who did not participate in the treatment program were found to be using psychoactive drugs. Dependence upon tranquilizers often begins during detoxification.

the amelioration of acute physiological malfunctioning and attempt to restore some measure of physical well-being to the alcoholic. Treatment in these terms includes a longer period of medical care, with a regimen of good nutrition, exercise, and a regular activity schedule.

As in the short term medical approach, the immediate goal of treatment is often attained. Upon discharge from the program, the basic health of the patient is much improved. Again, the effects of treatment are short in duration; the patients resume alcohol use within a short time and their health once more deteriorates.

The psychological model* of alcoholism minimizes the importance of physiological factors. But again, the unit of treatment is the individual; in this case the individual's personality system replaces the physiological system as the target for intervention. The alcoholic's drinking is here seen as the result of his faulty psychological make-up and treatment is directed toward changing his personality structure by means of one or two hours weekly of dyadic interaction with a psychotherapist.

This method of treatment is frequently as unsuccessful as a purely medical approach; so much so that many therapists feel that alcoholics are essentially unsuitable for psychotherapy. Those therapists who do attempt to treat alcoholics tend to accept only the youngest, most motivated, best educated, and most socially intact candidates; and even under these circumstances, treatment is often ineffective.

A number of state hospitals and private alcoholism hospitals maintain treatment programs based on a model which defines alcoholism as a psychological problem, but expands the definition of treatment to include longer term inpatient care. The range of treatment efforts in this type of setting extends from the same one or two hours weekly of individual psychotherapy used in the outpatient method (plus the benefits of a protective setting), to intensive *milieu therapy*. Psychoactive drugs may also be used, both to decrease the patient's discomfort and to make him allegedly more amenable to psychotherapy. This, as mentioned, may lead to the creation of a dual problem of drug and alcohol dependence. Inpatient psychiatric treatment often improves the patient's behavior and sense of well-being; but shortly

---

* We are aware that there are a number of psychological models; we speak here in terms of the most commonly encountered model.

after discharge, as in the case of other types of treatment, the majority of patients resume their former drinking patterns.

Two special treatment techniques which have gained popularity should also be mentioned here: Antabuse treatment and aversion treatment. Antabuse, administration of the drug disulfiram, effects a chemical change in the patient's organism such that the organism is rendered antagonistic to alcohol. The treatment is effective only as long as the patient continues to take the Antabuse every day, which is often difficult to insure. This treatment strategy involving long-term maintenance of the patient on a drug may produce unanticipated and undesirable physiological effects.*

Aversive conditioning attempts to change the psychological response of the patient by means of associative learning. Apomorphine, a drug which induces violent vomiting, is often used to produce such associations. Through repetitive experience, the patient develops a conditioned aversive response to the smell, taste, and sight of alcohol. This conditioned response, however, may be confined to the setting or context in which it was learned, without generalizing to all settings. And even when generalization takes place, the conditioned response seems to be short lived.

Both aversive conditioning and the Antabuse trials are also, in our view, humiliating and dehumanizing experiences.

The problem then with treatment approaches which define the individual as the sole unit of treatment is that they are unable to effect any lasting change in the individual. The alternative view is that the problem of alcohol misuse does not reside merely within individuals alone. It exists somewhere in the complex relationships between persons and their social contexts. Focusing upon the individual and searching for physiological and intrapsychic explanations for the individual's difficulties with alcohol draws attention away from the larger pattern and leads to ineffective treatment efforts.**

---

* Aside from effects on the central nervous system (drowsiness, headache, vertigo, etc.) there is a probable association between the use of disulfiram (Antabuse) and the occurence of peripheral neuropathy and optic neuritis. (*J Neurol Neurosurg Psychiatry, 34*: 253-259, 1971).

**This is not to deny that physiological vulnerability may constitute one part of the pattern, or that intrapsychic conflicts may complicate the picture.

Sustaining Forces for Alcohol Use

In the past, the larger social dimensions of the alcohol and drug problem were passed over as influences which were regarded as important, but which were not seen as the central question. We suggest that these social dimensions are more than influences and are, in fact, the most important constituents of the alcohol abuse problem. They serve to sustain it more effectively than does an individual's physiological tolerance or personal motives. Existing social patterns have recruited large numbers of persons into excessive alcohol use and social sequences for maintaining this use have become institutionalized.

For almost all members of American society, some form of alcohol use has become a regular component of personal self regulation and daily life. The use of alcohol, as well as of marijuana, tranquilizers and sedatives, has become an essential constituent of social interaction in which persons routinely participate. Mass and local media keep alcohol constantly in view and make it our daily companion.

The sustaining forces in the use of alcohol, therefore, do not reside within the individual alone, but lie in the whole context of events that sustain the individual's pattern of behavior.

Let us for a moment consider the difficulties faced by an individual who wishes to remain sober. His environment barrages him with messages containing the instruction to drink. The mass media carries many advertisements for alcoholic beverages. The alcohol industry, which contributes eight billion dollars in tax revenues, expends approximately two hundred million dollars annually for advertising. Every day the drinker is confronted by billboard advertisements and brightly colored neon signs displayed by bars and cocktail lounges. In many states even supermarkets and drugstores display alcohol conspicuously, often in locations such as checkout counters, which are unavoidable.

In addition to commercial influences, social pressures to use alcohol operate in most everyday situations. Drinking and alcohol is culturally associated with images of masculinity, sociability and hospitality. It is rare that one visits friends, attends a party or eats in a restaurant without being offered alcohol; and to refuse is often to create an awkward situation. In many occupations and social networks pressure to drink is especially intense.

Neither the alcoholic nor those attempting to help him are sufficiently aware of this powerful relationship between the drinking patterns of an individual and the influences forcing alcohol on him, which are ever present in the environment. This aspect of the problem is not perceived by treatment agencies or professionals. Their view of the problem is confounded by the *"dermal illusion:"* the idea that individuals are autonomous units in charge of their own destiny. One is reminded of the philosopher Spinoza's fantasy that a stone thrown into the air, and moving on a predetermined path to a preset landing point, would, if blessed with consciousness, believe that it was choosing its trajectory and landing site.

Many persons who have established a pattern of using alcohol and drugs and who are in social contexts where these agents are not only available but are pressed on them, are no more able themselves to effect a change in their use of these agents than can Spinoza's stone change direction.

Since a large part of the direction of the individual's behavior is determined by forces other than themselves, any attempt to change behavior must include attention to the significant influences upon it. It becomes evident then that an alcoholic's drinking pattern cannot be changed without making changes in his physical and social contexts.

The Special Status of the Alcoholic

The failure of the treatment of alcoholism further involves a number of other related factors. Alcoholics have in the past, and continue today, to receive harsh treatment from public officials and social agencies. Alcoholics are objects of scorn and derision; they have been imprisoned and institutionalized and subjected to verbal and physical abuse.

What explanations can we find for this widespread phenomenon? It has been suggested that the unconscious hostility of the alcoholic, his insatiable demands on those trying to help him produce a widespread negative counter reaction. We do not think that this psychiatric explanation helps in the understanding of the intractable bitterness and anger toward the alcoholic on the part of medical staff, officials high and low and the public at large. We suggest that a combination of factors are involved:

THE FAILURE OF THERAPEUTIC EFFORT. Medical personnel, not unlike most of us, are not well disposed toward those whom they have tried and failed to help. Failure threatens the desired self image of effectiveness and competence and one is likely to defend this image by blaming the object of one's efforts for the failure.

SOCIAL DISTANCE. In most treatment programs, alcoholics are frequently (though not always) lower in the social class structure than those who attempt to deal with them. Thus, they are subjected to the contempt and deprivation of genuine interaction by which social distance is maintained in everyday life.

EXPOSING THE UNDERSIDE OF THE AMERICAN DREAM. The alcoholic is perhaps too blatant a reminder of what our impersonal and disruptive social system does to a significant minority of its members.

THE CARICATURE OF NORMALITY. We are a drinking nation. The vast majority of adults and a sizeable proportion of minors, consume alcohol regularly. Though we would prefer to think in terms of qualitative distinctions, the drinking patterns of most alcoholics are but a quantitative extension of normal, socially accepted (and encouraged) patterns. Thus the alcoholic makes us more aware than we would prefer to be of hazards of the model of alcohol use promoted and subscribed to by the society as a whole.

DISRUPTION OF THE DERMAL ILLUSION. Finally, the alcoholic, by exhibiting an obvious lack of self control, disrupts the widely accepted illusion that each individual is autonomous, internally controlled, able to choose freely his course of conduct without regard for the social context in which he is embedded. Thus, the alcoholic threatens a basic tenet of traditional social epistemology.

Once the interrelatedness of environmental pressures and response is accepted, it becomes evident, however, that an alcoholic's drinking pattern cannot be readily changed without making changes in his physical and social contexts. The alcoholic must not only be extricated from contexts in which the message *drink* is present, but also be placed in a context in which another set of messages is dominant. No program can succeed unless it includes the development of new social arrangements, devised to provide positive human associations and territorial supports for those wanting to be free of the drug alcohol.

Chapter II

A COMPREHENSIVE MODEL

. . . in which we argue that the social reconstruction of the alcoholic's way of life is the most effective treatment strategy.

Alcoholism as a Function of Individuals and Their Social Contexts

IN OUR conception of alcoholism we begin with a disease model but then move beyond it. The individual disease model is partly appropriate, in the sense that some individuals who drink are not able to control their drinking behavior. Even after years of sobriety, exposure to alcohol will return some alcoholics to the addictive drinking cycle. (One of us has treated individuals with as much as twenty years of continuing sobriety who, upon being exposed to alcohol, have immediately re-entered the addictive drinking pattern with concomitant rapid physical deterioration.*)

---

* A number of investigators have claimed that it is indeed possible for some alcoholics to resume social drinking after a period of abstinence from alcohol. Foremost among these is Davis, who has maintained this position since 1962. And yet in a paper published in 1969 summarizing his own and two other studies, he can refer to only twenty-two cases in which this claim has been documented. On the other hand, many students of alcoholism wholly disagree with this claim. Ruth Fox, a life long student of alcoholism, states, in her experience with many hundreds of alcoholics, "I do not know a single patient of mine who has been able to resume normal drinking. Many of them have tried and failed. There may, of course, have been some who have succeeded in doing this, but if so I do not know about them. . . ."

Until the case for *controlled drinking* can be further documented, the weight of evidence tends to support the AA position that the only way to recover from alcoholism is to cease from any further consumption of alcohol. It makes as little sense to us to expect the recovered alcohol addict to be able to be an occasional social drinker as to expect the recovered heroin addict to shoot up occasionally without being drawn into the whirlpool of addiction.

In another sense, however, the individual disease model is incomplete and not wholly appropriate. Alcoholism is a health problem. Its course, whether progressive or arrested, does not depend solely upon what happens inside the victim of the *disease,* the alcoholic individual, but depends largely upon the personal and social surroundings within which he lives. Exposed to alcohol and to persons who drink, his *disease* is likely to take a malignant course. Surrounded by sober people, in social settings free of alcohol, the disease is likely to be arrested, allowing the alcoholic to lead a meaningful and productive life.

The more comprehensive view, therefore, asserts that continued alcohol misuse by vulnerable individuals cannot be arrested by attention to individuals alone. Alcoholism must be regarded as the result of a complex pattern of relationships *between* individuals and their social environments. A focus upon only the personal or chemical aberrations of the individual draws attention away from such a larger pattern and leads to ineffective and sometimes harmful treatment efforts.

Since a large part of the direction of the individual's behavior is determined by forces other than themselves, any attempt to change that behavior must include attention to the significant influences upon it. It becomes evident then that an alcoholic's drinking pattern cannot be changed without making changes in his physical and social contexts. He must be extricated from contexts in which the influence towards drinking is present and relocated in a social context in which other sets of messages are dominant. *The program* whose operations and effectiveness are described here, utilizes this strategy.*

The Social Reconstruction Model

What is needed then to genuinely aid the alcoholic is a new conception of treatment which goes beyond the misleading dichotomy of physiological therapy and psychotherapy. This model of treatment abandons the unrealistic goal of changing the individual alcoholic to fit the society in which he lives and seeks instead to change the

---

* The program developed under the auspices of San Joaquin Medical Facilities is known to its participants as Project FAITH (Furthering Alcoholics' Interests Toward Health).

social contexts in which he lives. Although treatment of the individual is necessary to restore the basic health of most alcoholics, this should not be thought of as treatment of his alcoholism, but only as treatment of its physical consequences.

Discarding the Notion of Cure

The starting point in the establishment of any treatment program for the alcoholic is the rejection of the assumption that alcoholism is a disease of the individual alone and that individuals can be *cured* of it. Since this notion is rejected, a program need have no time limitation on treatment; there is no point at which an alcoholic has completed treatment and is a "success" or "failure." Treatment is an ongoing process aimed, not at curing individuals, but at creating and sustaining for them a compatible social system. A by-product of this new orientation is that individual alcoholics are not considered to have failed if they resume drinking. They remain a part of their social system and are not abandoned by it.

Discarding the Why Approach

One of the conventional methods of psychotherapy* with the alcoholic involves the concept that one must probe into the alcoholic patient's past life to search out the root of his problem so that the patient can understand his disturbance and obtain insights which result in a change in his current behavior. Though some counselors and therapists working with alcoholics have now arrived at the view that alcoholism is perhaps neither a mental illness nor primarily a psychiatric disease, their therapeutic approach has not actually changed. Though they may no longer label the alcoholic as psychiatrically ill, their approach is exactly the same as it has been throughout the years.

If one listens to and observes these therapists working with alcoholics, one finds that the main theme of the interaction still revolves around the *why* question: "Why did you do this?" "Why did you do that?" "Why do you think about this the way you do?" And

* We are here describing one psychotherapeutic approach: the so-called "insight" approach. However, other psychotherapeutic approaches involve direction and manipulation.

therapists ask the alcoholic, "Why did you drink the last time around?" If the alcoholic gives an answer, the therapist then suggests that perhaps there are other reasons.

The rationale for this mode of treatment is that once the mysterious psychic aberration is uncovered, the alcoholic will be able to drink as other people drink, without difficulties. This conventional approach to the treatment of the alcoholic has been used for forty years with quite limited results; however, many therapists still cling to their basic beliefs in the traditional psychotherapeutic methods and resist change in working with alcoholics.

If one asks a group of nonalcoholics why they drink, the answers are fairly predictable: "Alcohol relaxes me," "It helps me unwind," "I like the effect," "It's a social lubricant," "It's difficult to say *no* when everyone else is drinking," and so forth. If one asks a group of alcoholic patients why they drank before alcohol became a problem to them, the answers are very much the same. However, if one asks the alcoholic patient why he drinks now that alcohol has become a problem to him, his answers are likely to be different: "Because I must drink," "to settle my nerves so I can get to work," "to keep from getting sick." He reports that alcohol now is like medicine to him and that he must have it to prevent the disturbing symptoms of withdrawal.

Thus the reasons why alcoholics drink are different from the reasons non-alcoholics drink, but the *why* of drinking changes only *after* the addiction to alcohol has developed. And it is not particularly helpful to know either set of reasons in attempting to change the alcoholic pattern.

Establishing Interpersonal Relationships

A basic goal of our program is the construction of a new physical and interpersonal environment for those it is treating, a landscape in which, as far as is possible, the commands* to consume alcohol are eliminated and a *counter-force* is created that contains commands not to drink. An important aspect of this landscape is a strong posi-

---

* We consider the presence of alcohol in private and public settings, as well as the advertisements for alcohol in the media and in public places to be potential *commands* to drink.

tive valuation of sobriety, repetitively communicated among all who occupy the landscape; sobriety is an accomplishment to be congratulated.

Another important feature of this landscape is that it contains alternative social forms and activities that make it possible and desirable to interact with others without the use of alcohol. The warmth and excitement of involvement with a community (in social and work situations) make the substitute satisfaction of alcohol unnecessary.

Education About Alcohol

While many alcoholics are self-educated experts on alcoholic beverages, they know next to nothing about the devastating effects of alcohol on the human organism.* Education about the reversible and irreversible effects of continued consumption of alcohol on the individual's mental and physical processes (specifically the brain, liver and kidneys) are considered a helpful element in the treatment of the alcoholic. Such education, however, seems most effective only in connection with the changes in the pattern of social life of alcoholics just described.

Our program, then, is based on a model which includes both the patient and his social context as units of illness and treatment. Both the patient's alcoholism and the circumstances and influences that direct it become targets for intervention. The object of treatment is not only to restore the patient to physical health but to help him remain sober by changing the social context and social networks into which he is returned. Concern is with the entire life space and context of the patient, both before and after he passes through the phase of medical rehabilitation (withdrawal from alcohol and physical recovery from alcohol related medical illness). Unless treatment is directed beyond the individual at one point in time, the efforts and resources invested in the medical rehabilitation of the alcoholic patient will fail.

Our purpose here is threefold: to describe in some detail an approach to the treatment of alcoholism developed at San Joaquin

---

* This failure for the alcoholic to be educated in the effects of alcohol on his organism are the more striking since he has had considerable exposure to medical settings and medical personnel.

County Medical Facilities (known as Project FAITH); to report the results of an evaluation of this program; and to describe those elements and strategies that we believe must be included in any program for the treatment of alcoholism which hopes to be effective.

It is our hope that the documentation of these principles will be helpful to those who are genuinely concerned with the problem of the alcoholic and that it will lead to a fundamental restructuring of treatment efforts.

Chapter III

THE PROGRAM:
ITS STRUCTURE AND OPERATIONS

. . . in which we describe the structure and contents of the treatment program and identify the stages of the recovery process.

Overview

Our program is located in San Joaquin County in California. At this time* it has been operating for approximately three years. It started as a pilot project with less than twenty clients in October of 1969, and by now more than 2,000 alcoholics** ranging in age from twenty-one to seventy-one years have participated in the program. Most have been alcoholics for many years, and many had been subjected to every form of treatment modality. Many had been jailed for alcoholism. While the program accepts both men and women, the vast majority of clients (almost 90%) have been men.

To get a more precise picture of the effectiveness of the program, information was obtained on every fourth person who had gone through the program up through March of 1972.*** Many of the persons selected for this review were known to the program staff, since they had continued to be active in the program; others were called or visited. Of those on whom information was available (n=205),

---

* November 1972.

** We are somewhat uneasy in referring to our clients as alcoholics, as if to imply that this label encompasses them wholly as individuals. The term is used here to describe persons who have become addicted to alcohol, and who often suffer serious physical consequences as a result of continued alcohol use.

*** We thought that it would not be a fair test of the Program's effectiveness to include recent alumni in the review.

seventy-eight percent were sober at the time of this follow up, and twenty-two percent were known to be drinking. However, information was not readily available on sixty-six persons.* It is likely that a majority of those with whom contact was lost are drinking, though a number are known to have moved to other areas of California or the country. If all of these are considered to be drinking, the effectiveness of the program would still be considerable (55%). However, we expect that some we could not reach in this follow up have remained sober. In a more intensive study of a smaller sample (eighty-six cases randomly selected) completed a year ago, 75 percent of those who participated in the program were found to be sober at the time of the follow up. Our conservative estimate then must be that the program has so far succeeded with about 65 percent of those who took part in it. Furthermore, the staff members familiar with those who returned to drinking point out that periods of sobriety for many of that group have been considerably longer since participating in the program.

Our program, as a whole, must therefore be judged to have considerable impact. We shall now describe its structure and the processes through which it enables individuals to recover from alcoholism.

Admission

In order to be admitted to the program, three requirements need be met. First, the candidate must be a resident of San Joaquin County. As a county supported service, our resources are limited to use by residents of the county. Second, only persons who describe themselves as having a problem with alcohol are admitted. No one is admitted who does not feel he has a serious problem with drinking, and no one is subjected to the program against his will. The third requirement is that the individual be able to commit three to five weeks to participation in the first, intensive phase of the recovery program. This first phase is carried on within a special facility at Bret Harte Hospital in Murphys, California, a village in the foothills of the Sierra, sixty miles from Stockton, California.

---

* Another thirty persons in our follow up sample had died since taking part in the program, testimony to the deadliness of alcoholism, and the often irreversible physical damage done by long term alcohol use! In the appendix we present brief portraits and cause of death for the thirty who died, and show how alcoholism kills young or old, male or female, black or white.

No one enters the Bret Harte* facility without being admitted by a program counselor. All counselors are sober alcoholics who have been through the intensive phase of the program. It is important to stress that the counselors are the mainstay of the program. Physicians and other personnel are available to assist with any medical complications that may arise, but the program is basically a nonmedical enterprise run by those it serves. San Joaquin County is one of the few places in the country where a lay person is empowered to admit an individual to a hospital.

Persons enter the program from several sources, most frequently the hospital itself. Alcoholic emergencies are monitored by the program staff and, as soon as possible, every individual admitted for alcoholism or alcohol related problems is visited by a counselor. Counselors make daily rounds in the detoxification service in the hospital (which is separate from our program) and explain the available alternatives to every patient. Counselors are also immediately available to those who walk in. Anyone who expresses a desire to stop drinking is given the opportunity to enter the program.

New members are also recruited from Starting Point, the Residential Detoxification and Care Unit described later in the book. Residents in that unit are regularly sent to Benton Hall, the building where our program is located, to discuss admission with the counseling staff and other members of the program.

A fourth source is direct referral. Public health nurses, social workers, and other service professionals in contact with alcoholics sometimes send someone directly to a counselor, anticipating that the person will subsequently be admitted to Bret Harte. Physicians may refer patients directly to the program.

As soon as a program entrant can travel, he is taken to Bret Harte Hospital located in Murphys, a small town in the foothills of the Sierra. He is given a bed in the ward, where he is cared for by staff and fellow patients, alike. Immediate support is provided by fellow alcoholics, and the new member is at once exposed to the larger context of the program. The effectiveness of the early stage is increased

---

* Bret Harte was formerly a tuberculosis sanitorium for residents of San Joaquin County. Its facilities have been converted to serve a number of special functions, such as the rehabilitation of the alcoholic.

when the alcoholic is introduced into the system in this manner, rather than after he has been fully detoxified elsewhere.

It did not take long for us to realize that caring for new patients, some of whom arrive in very poor condition, provides an opportunity for those who feel they are being helped to take care of someone else. In the view of the staff, this arrangement offers the additional benefit in that the new alcoholics coming to Bret Harte in serious condition (often undernourished, bruised, and injured) provide a living demonstration of the effects of alcohol. They serve as a reminder of what can happen. Thus, the social context is repeatedly peopled by individuals in the most distressing phases of an alcoholic episode.

Upon arrival at Bret Harte the person is introduced into a flow of activities that will continue through the phases of physical recovery, education, and involvement with fellow alcoholics. Each person enters the program at a different level of disability, and each one is dealt with accordingly. Every effort is made to minimize the use of psychoactive or tranquilizing drugs. It is a firm conviction of the staff that the administration of psychoactive drugs to alcoholics is dysfunctional in the long run, even though drugs may appear to yield short term benefits (such as reducing sleeplessness and irritability). This view is based on our observation that many alcoholics tend to substitute sedatives and tranquilizers for alcohol and frequently develop a dual problem of alcoholism and dependency on drugs.

The length of time spent at Bret Harte depends upon the person's and the staff's judgment of progress. Rather than instituting a formalized regimen of a specified number of weeks, each person is evaluated in terms of his individual rate of change. Some persons require much longer than others to regain full mental functioning. They remain in an alcoholic fog for some time, and the elements of the program cannot really begin to *take* with them until three or four weeks have passed. Others enter in better condition and are capable of participating fully from the outset.

Once clients arrive at Bret Harte, they enter into a round-the-clock program of education and interpersonal activity, only limited by their physical conditions. A variety of informational and social inputs is provided. Every effort is made to give the residents practice in developing and exercising new behavioral repertoires in relation to each other, and eventually to the world outside. The patient's progress can be described in terms of four interrelated stages, or phases. While these provide only the loosest framework for organizing the activities of the program, they supply a convenient way of following an individual through the intensive period of the program.

STAGES OF CHANGE

Physical Recovery

The first stage is that of physical recovery. The initial step in treating any patient is to help him through the physical problem of alcohol withdrawal. This period of detoxification and restoration to minimal physical well-being takes a few days, depending upon the person's initial state. Patients are not given intravenous fluids. The recent research of Beard and Knott has shown that alcoholic patients do not become dehydrated, as had long been assumed, but, on the contrary, become *over*hydrated.

Each entering patient receives a complete physical examination, including a chest X-ray and laboratory tests.

As mentioned, the acute distress of patients in withdrawal is not managed by physical means (such as the use of restraints) but is relieved by the presence of other members. Thus, a painful and frightening experience is utilized to strengthen the bonds of relationship within the program. (Physicians are on call to deal with possible physical complications.)

Mental Clearing

During the second phase some increase of intellectual functioning returns. This phase may take considerable time, since in many persons heavy exposure to alcohol impairs brain functioning to a great extent. Since they are most sensitive to alcohol, higher functions of the nervous system are affected most immediately. It takes considerably longer to clear *alcoholic thinking* than is generally realized. Symptoms and disturbed behavior may subside within a few days, but full mental functioning may not be restored for months. For some, changes are unfortunately irreversible. We have found that, on the average, patients will regain most of their mental abilities by the end of three or four weeks. By that time they are able to process the educational inputs of the program and are capable of absorbing and remembering their activities. The clearing process, however, is slow and gradual. Though this process starts with detoxification, it continues for months after patients leave the Bret Harte phase of the program.

Education About Alcohol

The third phase is that of education about alcohol. Education starts from the first day but often cannot *take* until mental functioning has been restored to at least some measure. A major goal of the program is to teach individuals about alcohol and its short and long-term effects. Such education is based on the premise that if the alcoholic is better informed about alcohol, he has a greater chance to survive without it.

Education takes many forms. For example, there is an initial lecture and discussion of four hours, augmented by slides and illustrations. In these the basic effects of alcohol on the human organism are described, explained, and documented. In a sense, alcoholics are taught who they are in this introduction, since the listeners exhibit many of the disorders described in the presentation. In addition, literature on alcohol and alcoholism is available in the program's library. Guest lecturers, most of whom are graduates of the program, also make periodic appearances at Bret Harte and at Benton Hall in Stockton. But a larger share of this basic education is carried out informally. The daily group meetings provide one occasion for this. The members gather together at least once each day to share their experience with alcohol. They are encouraged to inform each other about how their lives have been profoundly changed through their addiction to alcohol.

Continuing contact with the counselors is another source of information. Counselor are alcoholics with many years of sobriety. They share and explore many of the pitfalls which can lead to renewed drinking and demonstrate by the example of their own lives how to avoid them. Some lessons are difficult to accept. One basic message, reiterated over and over again, is that an alcoholic must change former friends in order to stay sober and must keep away from some features of his former environment. Certain jobs may be dysfunctional for maintaining sobriety (for example, bartender or salesman), and these must also be changed. What is passed along in formal and informal contacts is the aggregate experience regarding what influences and situations encourage people to drink and the news that concrete options are available, which provide alcoholics a chance to live differently than they have.

Continuous contact among program members is the final source of informal education. A number of small groups that develop informally are available all the time. At any hour of the day or night there is someone to talk to. There are no fixed bedtime hours. A good deal of the conversation is about alcohol and alcoholism. Along with the informational exchange, this easy access to social interaction is a most important element in the program.

The fundamental message of the program is that the person with an alcoholic problem is an alcoholic for life. The alcoholic suffers from a physiological impairment that does not permit him to drink without immediate, disastrous consequences. One can learn about one's condition and learn a variety of methods to avoid taking that first drink. Still the principal method of maintaining sobriety involves uninterrupted association with sober persons, and especially sober alcoholics. The alcoholic must renew his basic education about alcohol over and over again.

Reinforcement

The fourth phase in the rehabilitation of the alcoholic can be characterized as reinforcement. This stage lasts for the life of the alcoholic. Patients spend from three to four weeks as residents at Bret Harte. At that point they move on to live elsewhere, but they do not become *graduates.* For those who have undergone the initial phase of intense involvement with the project it is only the beginning; one never graduates from the program, nor is one ever cured of being an alcoholic.

When the time comes to leave Bret Harte, the resident, who is now a member of the larger fellowship, is immediately linked to a variety of organized activities that are very much a part of the total program. When a patient leaves Bret Harte to return to Stockton or elsewhere, he is frequently accompanied by another patient or a staff member, since this is recognized as a difficult transition point. Furthermore, no one is discharged from Bret Harte after his initial period of residence without having an appropriate place to go.

Unlike the vast majority of programs for the alcoholic, perhaps, our program does not see its responsibility as ending when the person "has gone through the program." A basic tenet of our approach is that whatever change takes place does not reside entirely within the person but includes every aspect of his life. The staff is especially concerned with the nature of the social context to which the person returns when he leaves. If he returns to the daily orbit which typified his life before his Bret Harte experience, he will more than likely drink again, no matter how positive his sojourn or how strong his new intentions. If he returns and succeeds in becoming embedded in a new social network, his chances are much better.

In Stockton, our program has developed a number of social environments which facilitate the association of sober alcoholics. There is a steady schedule of group meetings and social activities, such as dances and potluck dinners at Benton Hall and there are always opportunities to visit with former and present participants in the program and with the project's staff members.

New Developments

In the period of time since we completed the formal study of this program, it has continued to develop, principally by expanding and diversifying its interpersonal networks and territories. It has continued to move further from a medical model and has concentrated upon the relationships of the persons in the program to one another. In a natural process of following what succeeds, the project's social ventures have continued to grow.

TERRITORIAL EXPANSION: The territory of the program has now expanded beyond the physical boundaries of the San Joaquin General and Bret Harte hospitals into the community. For example, counselors now visit jails in the county to hold weekly meetings for alcoholic prisoners. This expansion was originally prompted by a desire to maintain continuing contact with the small minority of members who ran afoul of the law after entering the treatment system via the Bret Harte experience. It is in full accord with the principle of maintaining active contact with members under all possible circumstances.

Once this expansion began, however, it served the additional purpose of providing a gateway for new entrants into the program. At present, about two thirds of those who attend the group meetings in jail develop a substantial relationship to the program. Upon release, many enter the program, moving from the jail directly to Bret Harte.

NETWORK EXTENSION: The social network of the program has been extended to the families of members. This expansion has been accomplished through the establishment of two new weekly meeting forms, the Family Round Table and the Teen Table. These meetings not only serve the purpose of helping members' families learn to assist their alcoholic relatives; but they also serve to develop a strong relationship of all family members with the program. A weekly couples' meeting during the Bret Harte phase has also been added. The purpose here is to expand, strengthen, and diversify the larger social network within which each member is embedded.

NETWORK DIFFERENTIATION: As the network has increased in size, it has also become more differentiated, in response to the variety of its members' needs. Thus, a *repeater program* has begun at Bret Harte to serve those for whom the induction was insufficient to sustain sobriety.

Another development involves the establishment of monthly alumni meetings. At these festive dinners pins are awarded to those who have one or two (and soon three) years in continuous sobriety. These meetings additionally make real to newer members the possibility of continuing sobriety through association with the program.

INCREASING ANTONOMY: For any program oriented around the model of social reconstruction to develop successfully, it is necessary that it maintain the greatest feasible degree of autonomy from larger organizations with different structures and goals, such as hospital and governmental bureaucracies. Our program has been fortunate from the beginning to have achieved a good deal of independence from the larger hospital structure.

Recently, even more autonomy has been gained through the mechanism of legal incorporation, which allows many features of the program to be financially and structurally independent. For example, the corporation already manages the canteen system of the hospital and runs a patient day care center. Additional activities are being planned. Some of these are mentioned at the close of this chapter.

Goals and Strategies

The ingredients that ultimately account for the effectiveness of a program act in synergic relation to one another. The whole is thus more than the sum of its parts, yet the total process evades our grasp as we focus on separate components. We tend to think of treatment programs as being made up of components which merge together to form the total process. It is rather the other way around. A process unfolds day after day, and as observers, we abstract it, selecting legible dimensions of it to describe piece by piece. Again, it is the total process that is the effective unit of treatment. Separation into components is purely an arbitrary, though simplifying, operation. In the following discussion, we lift out of the flow of events a variety of activities carried on in the program. Our purpose is to describe the program, as well as to communicate information to those who may wish to put this model into action themselves.

The staff considers alcoholism a disease that can be controlled or arrested but cannot be cured. We hold to the premise that most persons who have become alcoholics cannot stop drinking by them-selves.* The major goal of the program is to assist the alcoholic through a variety of nontechnological means in refraining from taking that fateful drink.

In working toward this goal, a number of strategies have proved successful. These are beginning to emerge as a model of treatment of the alcoholic. We describe those we consider most important below.

Organizational Judo

The alcoholism unit at Bret Harte Hospital, together with its ante-cedent and subsequent extensions throughout San Joaquin County, practices what could be called organizational judo. Wherever a tech-nical or organizational stress point creates a potential problem, the program moves along with the force instead of putting up a resistance.

---

* This premise is, of course, that held by Alcoholics Anonymous, and one from which its method of operation proceeds.

A major asset of the program so far is that it has managed to make virtues out of necessities.

To illustrate, overcrowding on the unit is used to maximize contact among alcoholic residents. A deliberate effort is made to create a context in which the potential for ordinary human interaction is both maximized and encouraged. The potential disadvantages of crowding are balanced by permitting everyone complete freedom during his stay, both inside and outside the treatment facility. The many beds lined up next to each other at Bret Harte stand in contrast to the spaciousness of the environment just outside the door. There, a wide green lawn stretches out to the beautiful Sierra foothills.

Most of the details of running the treatment unit are assumed by the patients themselves, under minimal supervision from the counselors and staff. Maintenance activities provide patients with concrete responsibilities and an opportunity to do something for the unit, as well as to cooperate with others in performing the basic activities for their new *family*. As the program grows, more and more of the auxiliary activities of the medical facility are being taken over by the membership. For example, the kitchen at Bret Harte is partially staffed by program members, and the hospital canteen system is now managed and operated by the corporation.

The usual difficulties accumulating around rules and rule breaking have not been a problem. This potential source of problems has been dealt with by refusing to institutionalize many rules in the first place. (The major regulation which remains is that should a patient want to leave the grounds, he must sign out with the nurse.) No rules, no rule breakers. The management of behavior is the responsibility of everyone and is handled, in the main, on an interpersonal rather than an institutional basis.

When they are not specifically engaged in keeping their home up, ample opportunities for play (games), additional work, fishing, and person to person contact with counselors and other patients are available. The primary emphasis is on contact and conversation, because the patients have a good deal to talk about: their years of experience as alcoholics and what they are now doing to turn things around.

In contrast, most treatment programs, particularly for the alcoholic, are set up so that the patient is more than glad to be out when the treatment is over. Overcrowded facilities can be terribly uncomfortable and can make patients feel claustrophobic. Patients have little to occupy their days except for those moments when they get their treatment, whatever it may be. A key to understanding this contrast may be the fear of most treatment staffs that, should a program be too comfortable, patients may feel that they have found a *home,* a place they may not want to leave when their time is up. This could prove to be difficult where the goal is to move patients through a program as expeditiously as possible, returning them to their previous places in society. The very term rehabilitation means *to restore to a previous state.* Is this a proper goal for the alcoholic? Our answer is no. It is that previous state that is the principal problem.

The program staff does not fear making life too comfortable or making the patients too dependent upon one another. The more desirable participation in the program's activities appears to the patient, the better. Our strategy is to get alcoholics so involved with each other and with the program that they will not re-enter many of the environments which they previously occupied. Essentially, the program never lets go of its membership.

Construction of New Social Networks

The traditional goal of alcoholism treatment programs has been to change the alcoholic so that he will no longer drink or be able to drink, and then to return him to society. This view overlooks the fact that many alcoholics tend to be tremendously impoverished in their interpersonal relationships. As in most public health facilities, among the alcoholics participating in our program, 76 percent had been living entirely alone, and 56 percent had been unemployed. Most did not have friends, except for drinking buddies (and often not even this), and tended not to engage in social activities other than drinking.* This lonely and barren life is a human problem at least as severe as the alcoholic drinking pattern itself, and the two problems are certainly related in many alcoholics.

Both problems need to be attacked simultaneously. A collection of lonely, isolated individuals can be progressively transformed into an

---

* We do realize that alcoholism is no respector of socioeconomic class, and that there are alcoholics on every social level.

interdependent social network, capable of maintaining the sobriety of its members.

This process begins at Bret Harte, where alcoholics are brought together in an unfamiliar territory and deprived of their most common pastime, drinking. The similarities of the residents to each other are stressed, and the residents are defined as suffering from common problems, both physiological and social. They are encouraged to engage one another at many levels and in many settings, ranging from casual conversation to intense and emotional interaction in group meetings. The Bret Harte experience as a whole is defined as a cooperative group effort, in which active participation is encouraged. The interdependence of the group is continually stressed. Solidarity is further enhanced by references to the dangers of the *outside* society, both because of its normative demands for alcohol use and because of its misunderstanding of and hostility toward alcoholics.

At the close of three weeks, alcoholics, many of whom had become loners, isolated from others, now begin to feel and act together as members of a new protective and supportive system. When they return to Stockton or elsewhere they maintain these relationship bonds. The continued operations of the program are arranged to facilitate their involvement and interdependence with each other.

Reterritorialization

One major effort of the program is to reterritorialize the location and movement of its participants. One can think of the environment of the person coming to Bret Harte as an *alcoholic landscape*. The significant locations for social contact in that landscape (such as the bar district of Stockton) are designed for the procurement and drinking of alcohol. This routine pattern of the alcoholic's life is described by an orbit plotted for drinking. In a very real sense, the everyday landscape is saturated with opportunities and instructions to drink, and so long as the alcoholic remains part of that landscape, he cannot reasonably be expected not to drink.

Another feature of the alcoholic landscape is that it is filled with negative encounters and experiences, including down-and-out days and nights, police who arrest and jail alcoholics as bums, and doctors who treat them in the hospital with little more than an admonition that they had better do something about their drinking. The shift from the alcoholic landscape to the territories of the program reverses the trend. Persons are actively removed from what is for them a malignant landscape and become recipients of positive responses and physical comforts. Bret Harte provides at least a temporary respite. The comprehensive care given and the supportive environment act as a buffer. The impact of the alcoholics' former existence slowly lessens as he begins to participate in a new program of activities and to interact with a new set of persons.

What is important about the alcoholic landscape is not the availability of alcohol or the frequency of opportunities for its consumption, so much as the exclusiveness of activities revolving around the alcohol consumption. In reterritorializing the alcoholic, the effort is directed toward locating him in a more alcohol-free environment, to be sure, but the primary goal is to place him in a field where the strongest influences pull for involvement in human activities other than the consumption of alcohol. How is this reterritorialization accomplished?

Reterritorialization proceeds along two avenues. One involves a physical relocation of persons in helping them to change their daily environments and to adopt new patterns of social action. The other involves the reshaping of the symbolic meaning of the everyday landscape and the altering of the responses of the environment to the alcoholic. These two objectives form two aspects of a single process.

First, the alcoholic is extricated from his previous environments and is placed in a retreat setting for approximately a month. This literal removal is extremely significant. It appears that relocating someone for this period of time in a full range of daily activity elsewhere is tantamount to interrupting some basic momentum or trajectory and providing an opportunity for a new set of daily patterns to form. While at Bret Harte, patients are already sampling new territories and locations for human interaction. A variety of institutionalized social arrangements and activities exist for the membership. These include jobs, recreational activities, and opportunities for informal involvement with one another in addition to the regular meetings. Thus, while still fledglings, new members receive the opportunity to rehearse new roles and to familiarize themselves with a new turf.

The program has developed alternative settings for its membership. The effort is to duplicate what can be thought of as ordinary social settings and activities, but with one exception—the omission of alcohol. The membership is not sufficiently large to make this goal entirely feasible.

Second, in the new environment, the scale of responses to alcohol is altered significantly. In the ordinary landscape, sobriety does not call for positive feedback, yet, if one is seen drunk, one is responded to negatively. This places the alcoholic at a disadvantage. If he stays sober, at best he is responded to neutrally by the *normal* world. In the new landscape, however, sobriety takes on a new value. It becomes transformed into a positive act and is rewarded by one's fellows as such. In a *repeopled* landscape, the responses are shifted. Reterritorialization changes the values placed on routine actions and responses in the everyday world.

DIRECTIONS OF THE PROGRAM

Once we are clear on the model of behavior and change on which the program is based, the directions for further development of the program become clear.

DEVELOPMENT OF A COUNTER-FORCE: Influences compelling individuals toward drug and alcohol use are ever present in everyday life. They emanate from the mass media; they are carried by our friends and colleagues. Drugs and alcohol are intrinsic to most social settings and are pressed upon each participant with both good and bad intentions. It is difficult for the nonpracticing alcoholic to escape being enveloped by an alcohol environment if he participates in the routine aspects of social life, like everyone else.

Some therapeutic communities isolate their members from the larger community for long periods, if not forever, by creating a separate and private world, with limited reciprocal access and connections. The alternative strategy is to expand into the community, not as a collection of disparate individuals, but as a group whose members participate in most ordinary social contexts. For example, each alcoholic retains primary and real bonds with this community of sober alcoholics—that is, with individuals who have experienced the desolation of an alcoholic life and a literal resurrection through human relations. Yet each also participates in the everyday world as well.*

Such persons, together with others who understand alcohol and drug problems, will increasingly become a counterforce advancing attitudes and activities to counteract the myths and promotion of the prevailing alcohol and drug culture. Great strength is provided by a network of knowledgeable and responsible friends.

Future plans include the acquisition of additional living quarters (hotels, boarding houses) in locations where unskilled temporary jobs are often available. (Such job opportunities are one of the relatively positive features of skid row areas). We already have established an eighty bed residential facility that offers full room and board.

Inroads into the occupational world are being made. In addition to occupations within the structure of our program (which include jobs in the alcohol-free bars and hotel), training and employment within the larger economic system of Stockton are being developed.

It will be important for us to take leadership in the *reterritorialization* of the social landscape, first by creating alcohol and drug free territories and then by making them available to the larger society. Such a plan would involve the construction of both social settings and social forms. To be usable, these settings cannot be artificial but must fulfill genuine needs and functions. We hope that plans for the development of program-sponsored alcohol-free bars, stores, and coffee shops can be implemented.

Our objective is to increase the availability of settings in which friendly interaction unencumbered by alcohol and drugs is possible. In such territories sober alcoholic, ex-addicts, or others plagued by dependence on chemical inputs may feel a sense of belonging. Such settings can act as beacons of hope and reassurance. The social functions remain intact—only the chemicals are removed.

---

* There are quite obviously, in this approach, considerable similarities to the programs such as AA, Synanon and drug free community programs such as Phoenix House in New York. However, there are also differences. AA, for example, chooses to remain invisible and anomymous except to its members. Synanon emphatically discourages its members from returning to the larger community. Phoenix House, while exhibiting many similarities, faces, perhaps, a more difficult task of maintaining drug free *ex-addicts* in both worlds. The drug addict, as a rule, is disadvantaged, less skilled, and often less prepared to occupy the interface between a drug taking and a *drug-free* community.

Parallel to the enlargement of drug-free territories would be the reinforcement and adaption of social forms that permit social intimacy, joy, and excitement in living. As W. H. Auden has pointed out, the sense of festival, of celebration, of community, has all but disappeared from modern life. Many people are ill at ease and feel ill-fitted to encounter others in social occasions. Manipulation of oneself and one's relationships with others by alcohol and drugs is designed to produce festive and good feelings and make it possible for persons to relate to each other without fear, shyness or a sense of inadequacy. It will be necessary not only to allow persons to develop interpersonal skills that enable them to feel good and in contact with others without alcohol, but also to restructure such social occasions as parties and social gatherings of all sorts in such a way as to diminish the use of chemical agents.

The Residential Detoxification and Care Center

Until recently, detoxification was handled only in a special detoxification ward at San Joaquin General Hospital. The program has now developed an alternative to hospitalization or jail, a residential detoxification and care center.* The philosophy of the newly established center is one that makes it difficult for the alcoholic to get a sense of failure. In fact, it is anticipated that the arrangements made for the alcoholic or problem drinker during his stay at the center may often not work the first time.**

The center provides services for a variety of alcoholic clients who are suffering from long range effects of alcohol abuse, for individuals who are referred as drunk or as suffering from temporary effects of alcohol abuse, and for individuals who in the past have had alcohol problems and are in a temporary stressful or crisis situation.

The residential unit accepts self referred individuals, as well as those referred by law enforcement agencies, hospital emergency rooms

---

* The residential detoxification approach was developed and pioneered approximately two years ago by the Addiction Research Foundation in Toronto, Canada. The director recognized that medical treatment often did not prevent but even added to the revolving door syndrome. His program was designed and organized outside the medical system.

** The alcoholic may well rotate through the unit several times before an appropriate strategy is worked out for him or he begins to become involved in a treatment program.

(after medical evaluation), mental health clinics, Alcoholics Anonymous, and other groups and agencies in the community.

The staff evaluates each client to determine whether he requires a period of physical recovery to be provided by the center, whether he requires specific services which can be provided by other community agencies, and whether he will accept and could benefit from participation in the alcoholism rehabilitation program of San Joaquin County's medical facilities. Representatives from our and other recovery programs are available in the center; however, many clients do not commit themselves to programs until they have been detoxified at the center a number of times.

When intoxicated individuals are brought into a residential center which offers a climate of acceptance and understanding, they tend to recover more quickly, and the possibility of their developing more extended sobriety is greater. While there are no physicians, nurses, or medical personnel on the staff, the residential detoxification center does have medical back-up. In the event that there is a medical complication the alcoholic is immediately transferred to the hospital for care. In the Toronto Program, with three thousand admissions, only 5 percent of the clients needed medical intervention. Our experience after three months and approximately nine hundred admissions was very similar. The advantages of this kind of approach are numerous. First of all, it refers the drinking alcoholic to a staff with special understanding of alcoholism. It avoids medical intervention where medical intervention is not needed and thus allows physicians to devote their time to treating medical complications. It tends to decrease the indiscriminate use of tranquilizers and sedatives in the treatment of alcoholism. It provides a milieu of acceptance in which alcoholics feel comfortable and at ease. It puts the burden of responsibility for recovery directly on the alcoholic in that this program provides him the opportunity to become and remain sober if he so desires. It reduces inappropriate interventions which in the long run may prolong his drinking career. If the client chooses to leave the center and return to drinking, he is invited to return when he feels ready to do something about his problem. It affords the opportunity for recovery to many alcoholics, rather than to a select few who somehow find their way into hospital wards. Thus, it broadens the scope and makes available the necessary treatment to persons sincerely seeking assistance. The residential unit has been designed in cooperation with law enforcement agencies to receive alcoholics who otherwise would be incarcerated in jail.* We, of course, are in complete accord with the new legislation and are encouraged by the results of this redirection effort.

Drugs are not used in the residential center. Recovery is facilitated instead by person-to-person contact. Individuals in a toxic state from the effects of acute alcoholism are assured that someone is going to stay with them until they feel better. Meals are supplied, showers are available, and each person has a clean bed. As the alcoholic feels better, his individual needs are evaluated, and all of the services available in the community are explained to him. He can leave the center to attend AA meetings, for appointments at community agencies or treatment programs, employment, Salvation Army and so forth. He may then return to the Center and discuss his progress with his counselor. The counselor is not a rescuer; he only provides information. The Center is governed by an attitude of acceptance. Its program is not structured. The unit is locked but only from the outside; anyone can walk out at any time, and a few do.

At each admission a referral is worked out, and no one is encouraged to leave the Center without first having met persons from the community who can provide help or services. All of the ongoing programs and community resources that provide services to the alcoholic are outlined in a simple fashion which can be understood by the client. Clients are sent out into the community to make their own contacts with the resources which are available. If employment is a problem, they are sent to the agency that can provide jobs or information about jobs. If a medical problem exists, arrangements are made with an outpatient medical clinic or with a private physician. Representatives of Alcoholics Anonymous visit the center daily. If a client is interested in attending AA meetings, he is picked up in the evening and taken there. Every client is urged to make at least one contact with a community agency to initiate his own recovery pro-

---

* A new California law, which became effective March 4, 1972, does provide that if the county has a detoxification center alcoholics can be delivered there by the law enforcement agencies as an alternative to jail.

gram. Each alcoholic who stays in the Center has ample opportunity to meet, talk and interact with sober alcoholics, individuals who have had alcohol problems as serious, if not more so, as he has and who have yet managed to live with their alcoholism, maintain sobriety and lead constructive lives.

It is our hope that the time will come when general hospitals no longer have special detoxification wards. It does not make sense to segregate alcoholics in a special ward in a corner of a general hospital. After all, all other patients are admitted to general wards, irrespective of their diagnosis or disease. Since alcoholism is not a contagious disease, why indeed should alcoholics with medical complications be segregated? Alcoholics should be admitted to hospitals if they have medical problems that warrant admission. On the basis of the Toronto program and our experience at Starting Point, it should be recognized that 95 percent of drinking alcoholics can be detoxified without medical intervention and at least referred to ongoing programs. For a community to rely only on its medical facilities to treat alcoholics inevitably results in a revolving-door pattern.

A Note on Delirium Tremens at Starting Point

During the operation of the first six months of the non-medical residential detoxification center, there has been an unusually low number of clients who experienced withdrawal symptoms and D. T.'s. The counselors suggest several reasons for this phenomenon. One, though some clients do hallucinate, they feel free to talk about their bizarre visual experiences. Such free communication and trust shown to another person is not usually exhibited in medical detoxification units. It may be due to the fact that the counseling staff at *Starting Point* are recovered alcoholics and the clients are aware that the staff themselves have experienced many of the frightening experiencs of withdrawal. Reassuring the hallucinating patient and telling him of one's own experience appears to be a major reason for the rapid decrease of symptoms and the general well being of the client. Since there are counselors on duty on a twenty-four hour basis, the alcoholic in withdrawal is never isolated and therefore does not tend to panic when he experiences withdrawal symptoms.

Those of us who have worked within a medical model have been aware that the most difficult time to manage patients occurs during the night shift when the ward is quiet and lights turned out. This is the time of day when patients climb out of their beds, wander down the halls, and often display gross symptoms of withdrawal. In the residential setting, however, lights are left on at night and music is piped in so that total quiet does not occur. The continuous stimulation provided by individual contact, music and activities on the unit provides the essential ingredients to relieve severe withdrawal symptoms.

The seizure rate in the residential unit so far also appears to be much lower than in the acute medical unit. It may be that the clients in the hospital are still in a more serious physical condition. However, this alone cannot fully account for the low incidence of seizures in the residential unit, since many of these brought to the unit are chronic alcoholics. Again, it may well be the threatening character of a medical emergency setting that causes panic in many alcoholics. For this reason, visitors are not allowed in the residential care unit. Staff have observed that the presence of a uniformed officer or unannounced intruder may be followed by a seizure in one of the clients, sometimes even followed by a seizure in another client, as if a chain reaction had been set off. In a milieu of acceptance, without threatening persons or stimuli, alcoholics experience fewer symptoms and do not require vigorous medical attention.

Chapter IV

EVALUATION OF ALCOHOLISM TREATMENT PROGRAMS

. . . in which we deal with the errors and pitfalls in the traditional evaluation of alcohol treatment programs.

EVALUATIVE RESEARCH on programs for the treatment of alcoholics has usually fallen victim to the same inappropriate model on which the programs being evaluated are themselves based.

OUTCOME: The traditional evaluations of programs for the treatment of alcoholism have proceeded from the premise that the treatment has an outcome that can be classified as *success* or *failure,* or located on a continuum between the two extremes. This idea of an outcome as the culmination of treatment has seemed appropriate to researchers because it underlies the design of most alcoholism treatment programs. The conception of outcome is based on an analogy to the idea of cure and on a traditional paradigm of treatment as a process that ends at a certain point in discharge from the treatment program. Discharge has been considered the appropriate point at which to judge success or failure. It is, then, only an extension of the same model to consider the duration of cure and to do follow-up studies based on the notion of relapse.

The many evaluative studies which have been based on this model have contributed to widespread doubt about the effectiveness of alcoholism treatment programs. These studies consistently have concluded that while success of treatment at discharge (in terms of such indicators as withdrawal from alcohol, physical recovery and progress within the treatment program) is rather good, the duration of these cures is brief and the relapse rate is high.

In our view, both traditional treatment programs and traditional evaluative research are based on a model that is inappropriate. Our program cannot be evaluated in terms of this model at all, since most of its members are not discharged but remain, in some sense, in the program indefinitely. Thus, an evaluation of our program must reject the concept of outcome, except as a continuous process that begins with entry into the program and goes on indefinitely. It is to be judged in terms of changes in life styles, including sobriety, and the duration of these changes over time.

SUCCESS: We have suggested that the *cure* model is inappropriate as a basis for evaluating the effects of programs for the treatment of alcoholism. Rather, the effectiveness or success of a program is to be judged in terms of changes in the behavior and experience of those who are treated. However, when the notion of cure is discarded, another issue is raised: What is desirable change; who is it desired by; and what is it worth?

Desirable change may be conceived of as change toward a specified set of goals. One problem with this approach is that the goals specified may be unrealistic. For example, it has been considered desirable for the alcoholic to leave the treatment program at some point and to continue *on his own*. But this overlooks the fact that very few people actually do carry on on their own; all of us are maintained in our daily activities by the continuous support of family, friends, and co-workers. Many, though not all alcoholics, however, have few such persons awaiting them when they leave a treatment program. Yet if such interpersonal support is not made available to them, they will soon seek the substitute support of alcohol, with predictable consequences.

Unrealistic ideals are best avoided by defining desirable change in terms of improvement over a previous condition and over the condition of persons not treated by the program. We may choose *a priori* the changes we consider desirable, but we will not insist upon finding all of them.

In choosing which changes are to be considered improvements, judgment must be exercised. Maintaining gainful employment is a commonly used criterion in desirable change. It rests on the premise that it is desirable for all members of society to be economically productive. One problem with this criterion is that it is subject, among other things, to the influence of local economic conditions. At the time of this study, for example, the unemployment rate in the area of Stockton, in which our client population resides, was increasing steadily. The subjective satisfaction of the treated group, as measured by self-report, is another criterion, one that is commonly regarded with suspicion, but one that cannot be ignored entirely.

Abstinence from the consumption of alcohol is, no doubt, a most commonly used criterion of desirable change and one with which we agree. Still, some balance must be achieved when evaluating changes. Any change is necessarily related to other changes, and all must be considered together when a judgment of desirability is made. For example, if a patient stops drinking but becomes psychologically disturbed, has a desirable change been produced? On the other hand, if the client abstains from alcohol, aids in the rehabilitation of other alcoholics, relates to a network of new friends, and is subjectively happier and more self-confident, yet is not discharged from the program and does not find employment, we would still conclude that some desirable changes have taken place.

Treatment as an Intervening Variable

Traditional evaluative research does not examine treatment directly or determine the conceptual relationship between that which actually occurs in the treatment process and those behavior changes that are defined as outcome. Instead, *treatment* has a place in the research design only as an intervening variable of the *black box* variety. That is, the treatment itself is not considered important; only the effects of the treatment are. These are conceptualized as output from the black box.

In our view, however, the treatment situation needs to be closely examined so that we may understand which processes and patterns characteristic of the treatment tend to influence behavior. The treatment program is a new environment for the alcoholic, one that has both immediate effects upon his behavior, as well as other effects that appear later. When he leaves the program, the alcoholic must enter another environment with similar characteristics in order to sustain his new patterns of behavior.

The Client as Passive Recipient

The conception of treatment implied by the traditional model is that treatment is administered by a professional staff, which is active, to a patient, who is passive. This view is partly responsible for the attitude often espoused by staff that patients had better not remain long in a program. Within this framework, clients are seen as a drain on a program's resources.

In our program, however, those who remain for a period of time actually are a resource; they are directly involved in treatment of newer patients. Far from being a drain on the program, they are essential to it.

Successful and Unsuccessful Life Styles

Evaluative research commonly examines treated persons only in terms of their success or failure to meet the criteria of a cure. It does not usually seek to discover the differences in the life styles of the "successes" and the "failures" at the time of evaluation and to draw conclusions from this about the patterns of everyday life necessary for maintaining sobriety.

Whereas we are concerned with whether or not clients maintain sobriety, their abstinence from alcohol is not the only criterion by which the program expects to be judged. Unless the life style of the former alcoholic or addict changes drastically from a solitary life of social isolation to membership in viable social networks, we would consider the program ineffective. The value of such an outcome cannot be established scientifically. It represents the social and personal values of the persons who are developing and implementing this program of change.

Our program considers itself successful if it has succeeded in reversing the trend toward the personal, social and physical deterioration of the alcoholic; when its clients and members reestablish friendships and have the social skills to maintain them; when its members move more freely across the physical and social landscapes of the city and county without being attracted only to those settings in which alcohol is a way of life.

Chapter V

AN EVALUATION OF OUR PROGRAM

... in which we describe methods of evaluation and present data on the effectiveness of our program.

THE PROGRAM, as it has been described, evolved slowly over a period of months. A great deal of resistance had to be overcome to make possible a treatment program that differs so drastically and in so many respects from more traditional medical treatment programs for alcoholism.*

After eight months of operation, it was the impression of the staff that the program was making a unique contribution to the treatment of alcoholics. Staff members were in close touch with most of the persons who had participated in the program and were impressed by the extent to which the lives of many had changed. A majority of those who had been at Bret Harte had remained sober; some were working after many years of unemployment; and many were beginning to form useful and meaningful relationships, after decades of isolation and anti-social living.

While it was felt that there had been developed an important approach to the recovery from alcoholism, the staff was, to some degree, puzzled by the program's effectiveness and eager to determine which aspects and elements of the program were most helpful. Such an assessment was held to be valuable for future planning of services for alcoholics in our area and elsewhere.

Methods of Study

Our study of the alcoholism program of San Joaquin County began

---

* The kinds of administrative problems that had to be met may be of interest

with a period of observation. Evaluation research is often undertaken by researchers who have little understanding of the operations of the program they have been asked to assess. But members of our research staff lived at the Bret Harte facility for periods ranging from a few days to two weeks to observe the range of activities. They talked often and informally with most of the members of the staff and made systematic observations of clients and client-staff contacts at many times of the day and night. They learned as much as they could about the nature of the program from both staff and clients.

A major element of the research was to compare a sample of individuals who had participated in the program with a sample of alcoholics who had not. The names of persons to be interviewed were obtained from a list of all persons who had received treatment at the receiving and emergency services at the general hospital, in whose records the diagnosis of alcoholism had occurred. Two lists of names were compiled; those who had requested and been selected for the program and those who had not sought or had not been selected for the program. Every fifth person was selected for interview, and every conceivable effort was made to locate this person for interviewing. If it was not possible after considerable effort to locate an individual selected in the sample, the next name on the master list was substituted.

In addition to these two randomly selected samples we interviewed a special group of persons who had participated in the program and who, in the view of the program staff, had benefited significantly. This *special sample* included persons who now occupied responsible positions in the community. Their participation in the program, coming after a period of alcohol induced social and physical deterioration, enabled them to resume socially productive lives. A program has a right to be judged by its outstanding successes as well as its failures.

A total of one hundred five persons were interviewed in sessions lasting from twenty minutes to one hour.* Most were interviewed

---

only to those who wish to replicate this kind of program. We shall, therefore, discuss them in Appendix E.

* This study in depth was completed about one year before the less intensive review of a larger sample (three hundred cases) was begun. The overall findings of the more recent survey are reported on pages 36-38 of this book.

in their places of residence, no matter how far from the general
hospital. To locate some persons in the sample (especially the non-
program group) required repeated phone calls and visits, and sched-
uling that was arranged to be convenient for the interviewee. Not
until considerable unsuccessful effort had been made to locate and
speak to a person selected in the sampling plan was another name
substituted.

The Effectiveness of the Program

Note that the program chose to accept the majority of all those
who were seen for alcohol related problems at the San Joaquin
medical facilities. Initially, a number of criteria were established for
acceptance, but they have seemed increasingly less important, until
now, when the major criterion remaining is the willingness of the
alcoholic to participate in the program; that is, to accept the treatment offered. While the great majority of clients during the first year
of operation were "skid row" and working class alcoholics, the program has increasingly served alcoholics from a wide range of social
and economic backgrounds.

Patterns of Drinking

In our view a return to occasional or moderate drinking is not
possible for the true alcoholic. For him even a minimal use of
alcohol will in the long run have disastrous consequences. Therefore,
we do not consider that persons who are drinking have been treated
successfully. This does not, however, preclude their further participation in the program and its activities. Indeed, some staff members
believe that some alcoholics, by reverting to alcohol use, have to
demonstrate to themselves the truth of what they have learned during
their stay in the program.

Three-fourths of those who had participated in the program were
sober at the time of our study, in comparison with one-fourth of those
who had not participated in the program but who may have received
other help or treatment. (See Table I.)

With the exception of one person, for whom information was not
available, persons in the special sample had remained sober at the
time of the study.

TABLE I

ARE YOU DRINKING NOW?

	Sample (N=36)	Control group* (N=50)	Special sample (N=19)
Yes	25%	52%	0%
No	75%	24%	95%
Information not available**	—	24%	5%

* Control group here refers to alcoholics who did not participate in the program.

** Includes those who refused to answer.

Patterns of Working

About one-half of those who had participated in the program were employed either full or part time, whereas less than a fifth of those who did not go through the program were working. Most of the respondents in the special sample were employed, though not all were paid for their work. (See Table II.)

Some of the respondents in the Bret Harte sample and more in the special sample either worked for the program or were engaged in activities directed toward helping the alcoholic. For example, one member of the special sample was the manager of the Benton Hall Annex, a living arrangement established by the program for alcoholics who leave Bret Harte and who have no suitable place to go. Alumni of the program are discouraged from returning to the rooming houses and hotels where they formerly lived. Another of the respondents in the special sample had set up a boarding house for members, which also served as a setting for group meetings and for

TABLE II

DO YOU HAVE A JOB NOW?

	Sample (N=36)	Control group (N=50)	Special sample (N=19)
Yes, full-time	28%	12%	58%
Yes, part-time	22%	8%	11%
Unpaid work	12%	2%	5%
Not working	38%	66%	27%
Information not available	—	12%	—

alcohol-free social gatherings. It is quite logical that the program re-
cruits its staff from among its successful members and that some individuals who have experienced the life of the alcoholic and who themselves narrowly escaped the destruction of their physical and social
selves will wish to work in the treatment of alcoholism or in providing services to the alcoholic.

Patterns of Everyday Life

An explicit objective of the program is to change not only the
alcoholic's drinking behavior, but also the style of his everyday life.
Indeed, unless the fabric of the social life of the alcoholic does undergo
serious changes, his chances of remaining sober are slim. In our research, we therefore inquired about housing and living arrangements,
as well as about the kinds of social associations maintained by the
respondents. (See Table III.)

TABLE III
WHERE ARE YOU LIVING NOW?

	Sample (N=36)	Control group (N=50)
Private home or apartment	56%	64%
Boarding house	19%	4%
Hotel, rooming house	3%	14%
Special housing arrangements (including Benton Hall Annex and Benton Hall)	14%	2%
Institution (including jail and state hospital)	3%	8%
Not ascertainable	6%	8%

There were some differences in the types of residence occupied by
the alumni of the program and by other respondents. Alumni tended
not to return to hotels or rooming houses, but lived in boarding houses,
or stayed for a while in special housing arrangements provided by
the program. However, the largest number of respondents in both
samples resided in their own houses or apartments. The major difference between the two groups was, however, not where they lived,
but with whom they lived, whether they lived alone or with one or
two friends or with a group of other people. (See Table IV.)

More than twice as many alcoholics who did not participate in the

TABLE IV
WITH WHOM ARE YOU NOW LIVING?

	Sample (N=36)	Control group (N=50)
Alone	17%	32%
With spouse only	34%	18%
With family	20%	34%
With 1-2 friends	11%	2%
With group	20%	4%
Information not ascertainable	—	10%

program lived alone, than did alumni. This difference, as we explained earlier, is probably considerably larger than it appears in these figures, since we could not locate many who had originally been selected for the sample of the control group. Among those we could not find were probably many who had no regular housing arrangements, who slept in the open or who were on the move from one city to another. While almost a third of the alumni (31%) lived with one or more friends, only 6 percent of the control group did so.

The answers to the question, "With whom are you now living?" quite clearly distinguished the two groups.

Patterns of Social Interaction

If the objectives of the program are being met, we should expect to find the most significant differences of all in the patterns of social interaction and social relationships of the sober alcoholic. From what we have seen of the operations and the philosophy of this program, it is the social group and the new social networks and associations that support the alcohol-free everyday life.

Table V documents the differences between the patterns of social interaction of individuals who have participated in the program and those who have not.

For example, 72 percent of the control group spent much of its leisure time in solitary activities, compared to 34 percent of the program alumni. 46 percent of the control group respondents spent time in solitary activities (characterized as nonproductive), such as drinking and watching TV, compared to only 18 percent of the program alumni.

TABLE V
How do you spend your spare time?

	Sample (N=36)		Control group (N=50)	
Solitary nonproductive	18% ⎫		46% ⎫	
		34%		72%
Solitary productive	16% ⎭		26% ⎭	
Interaction-seeking	10%		6%	
Interaction recreation	10%		5%	
Interaction within special settings	20%		3%	
Interaction with other alcoholics				
at group meetings	18%		2%	
Other	4%		11%	
Number of responses given	79		61	
Average no. of activities listed	2.2		1.2	

A considerable amount of the social interaction of alumni revolves around sober alcoholics, in informal and formal group activities and settings. These activities occur to a large extent within the framework provided by the extensions of the program in Stockton, at Benton Hall and Benton Hall Annex. In addition to participating in group meetings, the alumni visit with staff and other alumni and engage in a variety of social activities with them, which include Sunday potlucks, and alcohol-free New Year's Eve parties.

Drugs and the Treatment of Alcoholics

In many programs alcoholics are frequently encouraged to take psychoactive drugs (sedatives, tranquilizers, stimulants). Physicians prescribe these drugs to relieve the symptoms of alcoholism (such as insomnia, anxiety, jitters, and non specific pain). Pharmaceutical companies have recently undertaken extensive campaigns to assert that drugs such as Serentyl are the treatment of choice for the alcoholic. Alcoholics themselves have learned to substitute sedatives and tranquilizers for alcohol when it is not available or when the social context makes it impossible to drink. Often, they become dependent on both alcohol and drugs and use them concurrently. However, alcohol and many drugs such as barbiturates are lethal when taken together, and their continuous use not infrequently leads to accidental overdosages and death.

Our program at its outset adopted a policy that restricted the use of psychoactive drugs to the initial phase of withdrawal and the first week of treatment. After that patients are taught to abstain from pills as well as from alcohol, though they do receive medication for somatic conditions like glaucoma and arthritis. Only one-fifth (19%) of our patients were taking tranquilizers or sedatives at the time of our study. Thirty-eight percent of the control group was using psychoactive drugs, while another 18 percent did not provide information on its drug taking. (See Table VI.)

TABLE VI
ARE YOU TAKING ANY MEDICATION NOW?

	Sample (N=36)		Control group (N=50)	
No (or vitamins only)	50%		34%	
Only for somatic treatment	25%		10%	
All psychoactive drugs	19%		38%	
tranquilizers		12%		23%
sedatives		7%		13%
stimulants		—		2%
Information not available	6%		18%	

Some pharmaceutical companies are now developing aggressive campaigns (by advertising in medical journals and by direct mail to physicians) advocating the use of drugs for the alcoholic. The policy of our program with regard to drugs is clear. Tranquilizing drugs, both minor and major, are seen as contraindicated in the treatment of alcoholism because their use compounds the very problem for which they are being prescribed. They reinforce the false view that the problem is the individual, his chemical or psychological imbalance, and their use involves the real danger that the patient who is to be helped will eventually come to be addicted to both drugs and alcohol for the management of his everyday life.

A Note on the Social Isolation of the Alcoholic

We gathered considerable information on the isolated and solitary life patterns of the alcoholic individuals in our sample. To make certain of the accuracy of this description, we also collected some basic information on the characteristics of all persons admitted to the receiving and emergency services of the general hospital for a nine month period with a diagnosis of alcoholism or an assertion of an alcohol problem.*

During a nine month period there were six hundred patients who met the criteria. This figure included mostly persons in an acute physical crisis brought about by the use of alcohol, but it represents only a fraction of the patients with alcohol-related medical problems at San Joaquin General Hospital.

These six hundred patients were preponderantly male, white (81%), and over forty years of age (82%). Sixty-nine percent of the men and 40 percent of the women were living alone at the time of admission to the emergency services. Of the remainder, most lived in small household units involving only one other person each. These figures, concerning a large number of patients, are further documentation of the social isolation of the alcoholic. He is most often an individual bereft of social ties, without group or network supports.

An event that occurred in the spring of 1971 provided a sad commentary of this thesis. During the early stages in the writing of this book, there appeared a news item reporting the deaths of more than twenty men in Yuba City, California, murdered over several months. One of the most significant aspects of this tragic event to us was the fact that, though these men had disappeared, there had been no inquiries about them during those months. The men were described as drifters, migrants, and probably alcoholics. At some point these men may have had families, parents, spouses, children, co-workers and friends. At the time of their deaths they were so disconnected from social networks that they were not missed.

The only human contacts available to many alcoholics are those made during the act of drinking with other alcoholics in places where alcohol is bought or consumed (bars, liquor stores, and public places

---

* (There was little doubt about the accuracy of the description of most of the patients, since they had received emergency treatment on many occasions during the same year.)

such as parks). One objective of this program is to reconnect alcoholics with a new community and a new social context in such a way that their absence will be noted and their fate will become a matter of concern to the other members of this community. Any program that does not recognize this central fact and does not attempt to reconstruct the social landscape of the alcoholic and reconnect him to meaningful human associations has, in our view, little chance of success. Our program builds its purpose upon this recognition. This, in our view, is a major reason for its effectiveness.

Evolution of New Social Networks

The time spent at Bret Harte is crucial for the development of relationships among the neophyte members. Bret Harte is the locus of entry into the program. It is there that, within three to four weeks, alienated and isolated individuals must become interconnected to form a mutually supportive system capable of sustaining the sober well-being of its members. Much development must take place in this intensive setting to produce ties that will survive transfer to the less intensive settings in Stockton.

In order to understand the evolution of interconnectedness more clearly, we have systematically observed the fabric of everyday social interaction among new and old members at Bret Harte. Several members of the research staff have spent varying periods of time actually living at Bret Harte and participating in all aspects of day to day life there. From this participant observation we learned about several stable, repetitive elements of social experience among those residing at Bret Harte.

The following elements together served to facilitate interaction among new members:

1. *Encouragement of verbal interaction*: One of the most consistent, recurrent messages heard at Bret Harte is, *talk to people.* Staff members and more senior members of the neophyte group (who themselves may have been at Bret Harte three weeks) offer continuous encouragement to new members to engage in conversation.

2. *Lessons in interaction*: Staff members and more senior members not only encourage new members to interact, but also spend time with them and in effect teach them how to interact, what to

talk about, how to improve their style of relating, and so forth. Many alcoholics who have for some time previously lived alone and in a milieu in which their social skills have tended to atrophy begin to rediscover or even to discover for the first time the pleasures of sober social interaction.

3. *Settings for interaction*: The physical environment furnished by the Bret Harte cottages facilitates interaction. Cottages get rather crowded, though not uncomfortably so, and have few partitions. So it is rather difficult not to be within interactional proximity. The comfortable and cheerful social areas also contribute to this end.

4. *Activity structures*: Interaction can be initiated and continued much more easily if a mutually understood conventional structure is used to guide it. Such structures as card games, ping pong and pool are used for this purpose at Bret Harte. Other structures that are used include the more ritualized format of some of the group meetings, and the informal ritual of an exchange of personal history.

5. *Time*: Last but not least, there is time for interaction. The day is not so heavily programmed as to discourage informal inter-action and not so underprogrammed as to exhaust the resources of this mode of interaction or produce boredom.

All aspects of everyday life at Bret Harte are different from the isolation of an alcoholic's old activity patterns: the purposefulness of twenty-four hours a day immersion in a heterogeneous human en-vironment produces the amount and variety of interaction necessary to the development of stable relationships.

Systematic Observation of Interaction

In addition to the general and rather informal staff observation of living at Bret Harte, procedures were developed for the formal monitoring of patterns of interpersonal involvement. For a number of days, at set periods throughout the day, staff members recorded who was interacting with whom in each of the living areas. They also observed at each meal and each group meeting who was sitting with whom. From these samples of interactional behavior *patterns of inter-connection* were constructed for the group as a whole. These patterns of interconnection resembled traditional sociograms (pictorial charts of relationships) but were based upon direct observation of recurrent interaction, rather than upon interviews.

Follow-up Study of Observed Networks

Analysis of the patterns of interconnection derived from our observations at Bret Harte allowed the delineation of subgroups, small and more intensively interactive networks within the larger network. Approximately three months after the period of initial observation at Bret Harte, we attempted to recontact in Stockton all those we had observed. There were two reasons for doing so. The first was to ascertain whether our observations of recurrent interaction corresponded accurately with the experiences of the individuals observed. Therefore, we asked each of those we contacted who had been his closest friends at Bret Harte and whether those relationships had continued to the present. In most cases, conclusions from the observational material were confirmed by the interviews; those who had been repeatedly observed in interaction with each other regarded each other as friends and had often continued the friendships after their return to Stockton.

The second purpose in following up the subjects of the observational study was to discover how well they were doing. We found that many of those who did maintain their sobriety had belonged to the same small networks at Bret Harte; several twosomes and three-somes that had developed at Bret Harte were found to be sharing living quarters. Some of those who did *not* maintain their sobriety also were members of small networks at Bret Harte, but in those networks everyone returned to drinking. Some formed no network relations at all while there, and these clients, too, tended to resume drinking.

These studies provide still more confirmation of the notion that the development of interpersonal relationships is central to the successful operation of the program and to the maintenance of sobriety in general. However, a warning can now be added: not every relationship will serve this purpose. It seems that some of the small networks that developed at Bret Harte had the primary function of insulating and isolating their members from the rest of the population and from the processes and messages designed to promote sobriety. Interaction among members of these *negative* networks was not usually continued after leaving Bret Harte, and almost without exception, the members of such networks resumed their alcoholic drinking patterns within a short time.

A note on the disruptive effects of observational studies on treatment programs, also is warranted here. Though 75 percent of the sample as a whole had maintained sobriety since becoming involved in the program, a smaller percentage of the persons more intensively observed for a two week period at Bret Harte had done so at the time of follow-up. It seems likely to us that the presence of data-gathering observers during this crucial initial phase of treatment may have reduced the effectiveness of the program somewhat.

TABLE VII

WHICH PART OF THE PROGRAM IS MOST IMPORTANT?

	Sample (N=38)	Special Sample (N=19)
All equally important	45%	32%
The group meetings	18%	11%
Lectures	13%	5%
Being with others with the same problem	8%	11%
Counselors	8%	11%
Nurses	3%	5%
Being away from Stockton	3%	11%
All staff members	3%	5%
Information not ascertained	—	11%

When we draw conclusions only on the basis of those who were willing to single out one element as the most important, we find the following:

Most of those interviewed considered it crucial to be grouped for treatment with others who had alcohol problems. "They are the only ones who understand. We had a common bond," said one. "We realized our problems together," "I saw things in them that made me see myself," said others.

Group meetings were considered an essential aspect of treatment, and they were named most often as the most important part of the program (by 29 percent of those who attempted to answer this question). "Good to unburden yourself and gain confidence" and "That is where I learned how to deal with my problem" were typical comments. The three hour educational lecture on alcoholism was described as enlightening. The program counselors were described as helpful, sincere, and down to earth; several persons interviewed said they considered it especially advantageous to be helped by others who "have had the same problems." One especially supportive female counselor was most often singled out for praise, and the most direct of the male counselors was often praised but also criticized by some for "coming on too strong." The doctors and nurses in the program were also described as "beautiful people, skilled, hardworking, and not standoffish."

The isolation of the treatment setting was considered an advantage by most; but 30 percent of those interviewed said that this aspect was of little importance and a few disliked it.

A majority of persons interviewed considered the minister and the religious program helpful. However, the personal qualities of the minister (his warmth, his social facility, and his status as a well-functioning handicapped person) were considered more helpful than his formal religious role.

A Study of Members Who Returned to Drinking

Our hypothesis concerning the change in life style necessary for the maintenance of sobriety received further confirmation when we examined the life styles of those members who had resumed drinking.

In contrast to the 75 percent of the members who were maintaining their sobriety, those who had resumed drinking had altered their previous life patterns far less (see Table VIII). Seventy-eight percent of the drinking alumni were still living in housing they had occupied before entering the program; none were living in the special housing arrangements developed by the program. None were living with their families, and only one was living with a group of friends. Thus, their everyday territories were not conducive to the maintenance of sobriety; they were still isolated and without interpersonal support.

Compared to the sober alumni, the drinking alumni of the program had much more empty time. Only one person in this group had any sort of employment whatsoever. They named substantially

TABLE VIII

COMPARISON OF SOBER AND DRINKING MEMBERS OF THE PROGRAM.

	Drinking Members	Sober Members
Have not moved since joining program	78%	40%
Living in special alcoholics' housing	0	30%
Living with family	0	22%
Employed (includes unpaid employment)	11%	24%
No. of spare time activities named	1.4	2.2
% of activities involving sober alcoholics	23%	40%
Attend alcoholics group meetings	56%	92%
Average no. of meetings attended per month	5.8	14.6

fewer spare time activities, and the activities they named were ones unlikely to involve the company of sober alcoholics. Finally, the drinking members attended alcoholics' group meetings only one-third as often as did sober members; almost half of the drinking group did not attend any group meetings at all.

It seems clear from an examination of these differences that a treatment program for alcoholics is successful only when it facilitates basic changes in the alcoholics' life styles, in their interpersonal relationships, and in their daily orbits of activity. If these changes are not accomplished, drinking patterns are unlikely to change.

Summary of Evaluation

The evaluation of the effectiveness of our program reported here began about one year after the inception of the program. Our findings, based on a random sample of participants and a random selected control group of alcoholics,* document our subjective impression of the impact of the program on its participants.

1. Only one-fourth of those who had participated in the program were drinking at the time of the study, although many of those who were sober had histories of alcoholism of many years duration.

2. None of the members of a special sample (a sample of alumni, who by consensus, had benefitted greatly from the program) was

---

* Though the number of cases selected (for comparison) are small, they were selected on a strictly random basis, with every effort made to meet the requirements of the design. The findings, therefore, should, within a small margin of error, reflect the effect of the program as a whole.

drinking at the time the interviews were conducted, and all remain sober at this writing.

3. The program dramatically changed the pattern of everyday life for many alumni. More than half were employed; few were living alone.

Recommendations

On the basis of our experience we offer a set of recommendations for the development of a sound treatment program.

1. Medical treatment and social rehabilitation should be integrated in any alcoholism treatment program initially; however, as the need for medical care decreases, the social reconstruction process should become dominant in the ongoing program. Although some patients are not very receptive to a social treatment program in the earliest stages, they can be given some exposure to it, so that it will not seem a strange, disconnected experience initiated at a later date, but rather a continuous part of the total treatment. If the same staff is involved in both types of treatment, still more continuity is gained.

Treatment of the physical consequences of alcohol use alone is not a solution by itself; it only produces the revolving door syndrome and is solely an expenditure of medical resources. Medical intervention can be inappropriate if the goals of recovery are too short sighted.

2. Alcoholism treatment programs must give more than lip service to the notion of alcoholism as a chronic, incurable condition. Patients should be educated about their physical condition and limitations and about the changes they must make in their lives to control the condition and to maintain health.

3. The personnel of alcoholism treatment programs should be educated about alcoholism. Most medical and health personnel are poorly informed in this area and often have the layman's view of alcoholism as a moral weakness whose treatment is doomed to failure. The attitude of medical staff may be even more pessimistic than that of the layman, because of their past experiences in revolving door alcoholism treatment facilities. Health care professionals must learn that treatment can be successful, and the best way to accomplish this is by demonstration. Visits to successful programs are helpful, as are discussions with sober alcoholics.

Sober alcoholics who have been through programs such as ours have an intimate, experiential understanding of the addiction and treatment process that can rarely be matched by health professionals. For this reason (as well as others), it is advisable to have sober alcoholics as members of a treatment team. (Alcoholics have been employed in other programs, but usually as low status assistants, rather than as full fledged members of the staff, whose experiential understanding complements and enriches the understanding of the professional staff.) Sober alcoholics are also valuable as staff members because they can relate more comfortably and spontaneously to alcoholic patients than professionals and can act as realistic role models with whom the patients can identify.

4. Alcoholism is not solely an attribute of the individual; it is reinforced by a pattern of relationships between the individual and his social contexts. These social contexts must be manipulated to facilitate changes in the individual's drinking behavior.

Certain minimal social conditions may be considered virtually essential to the maintenance of sobriety. These include:

a. frequent association with sober alcoholics;

b. nonsolitary living arrangements, preferably with other sober alcoholics;

c. occupation of some sort, either employment or leisure activities (helping in the rehabilitation of other alcoholics is especially desirable); and

d. participation in social activities while sober.

The conditions cannot be achieved merely by telling the alcoholic to change. The treatment program must implement his changes by providing facilities, organization, and encouragement.

5. Care must be taken in arriving at criteria for evaluation of a treatment program. Success is often an all or nothing proposition; the alcoholic who resumes drinking is most often in the same condition he was in before treatment. Yet, too stringent criteria may result in the labeling of many patients as failures, thus lowering the morale of both staff and patients.*

---

* Though the goal of our program is sobriety, alumni who go back to drinking are encouraged to re-enter the program. Although the program failed the first time, the alcoholic is not considered a failure.

SUMMARY

ALTHOUGH THE VIEW is at last becoming widely accepted that alcoholics need and deserve some form of treatment, the response from our health care systems so far has been to attempt to force alcoholism treatment into the mold of established medical and psychiatric treatment models. The existing models, as a rule, are based on the incomplete premise that alcoholism is a disease located wholly within the individual alcoholic.

Acceptance of this premise leads to treatment efforts aimed at producing some physiological or psychological change within the individual, such that he may after some limited period of time be discharged from treatment as cured and henceforth have no problems with alcohol.

The majority of alcoholism treatment programs are alike in their adherence to this basic model. The differences between programs result from varying assumptions regarding the individual's disease and the appropriate strategy for producing change in him. The dichotomy in treatment programs is between those which concentrate on physiological operations, including chemotherapy, and those which stress psychotherapeutic operations. In our view the distinction between the main types of major treatment orientations current today is a small one, and both are limited in scope and in comprehension of the problem.

The alternative view that we are suggesting is that the problem of alcoholism does not reside entirely within individuals and that it cannot be solved by attention to individuals alone. We believe it exists somewhere in the complex relationship of persons and their social contexts. Focusing upon the individual and searching for metabolic or intrapsychic explanations of his difficulties with alcohol may draw attention away from the larger pattern and lead eventually to ineffective treatment.

A consideration of genetic, biochemical, and metabolic factors is crucial to an understanding of who becomes an alcoholic. However, once the alcoholic disorder has been established, the problem must be conceived of in terms of another model emphasizing social processes.

Therefore, the individual disease model is incomplete and not wholly appropriate. Alcoholism is a condition whose course, whether progressive or arrested, does not depend solely upon what happens inside the victim of the disease, but depends largely upon the personal and social surroundings within which he lives. Exposed to alcohol and to persons who drink, his disease is likely to take a malignant course. Surrounded by sober people in social settings free of alcohol, the disorder is likely to be arrested, allowing the alcoholic to lead a meaningful and productive life.

The more comprehensive view, therefore, asserts that continued alcohol misuse by vulnerable individuals cannot be arrested by attention to individuals alone. The sustaining forces in the use of alcohol lie in the whole context of events that regulate the individual's behavior.

Programs for the treatment and rehabilitation of the alcoholic must consider how difficult it is for persons already habituated to an alcoholic way of life to remain sober within an alcoholic society. Once the relationship between environmental pressures and response is accepted, it becomes evident that an alcoholic's drinking pattern cannot be readily changed without making changes in his physical and social contexts. He must be extricated from contexts in which the message *drink* is present and placed in a context in which another set of messages is dominant. No program can succeed unless it includes the development of new social arrangements, devised to provide positive human associations and territorial supports.

The starting point in the establishment of a treatment program is the rejection of the assumption that alcoholism is solely a condition of the individual; that individuals can be cured of alcoholism. Once this notion is rejected, a program need not limit the duration of its involvement with the person; there need be no point at which an alcoholic has completed treatment and is judged a success or a failure. Treatment then can be an ongoing process aimed at creating a new social landscape and at reconnecting alcoholics with a community concerned with their well-being.

A basic goal of any such program should be the creation of inter-connections among those who are being treated. It is difficult, but nevertheless possible, to create such a community if one has the proper understanding of the task to be done. The notion of patients' being helped by the professional staff is replaced by the notion of all those being treated helping each other in a continuous ongoing process. What the alcoholic needs is not time-limited treatment, but relationships with people in a social network that is able to maintain the sobriety of its members.

In our program this process begins at Bret Harte Hospital, a residential treatment setting separate from the hospital at which the alcoholic first seeks help. There alcoholics are brought together in an unfamiliar territory and deprived of their most common pastime, drinking. Their similarities are stressed; as alcoholics they are defined as suffering from common problems, both physical and social. They are encouraged to interact together at many levels and in many settings, ranging from casual conversation to emotionally charged group meetings. Their meeting at Bret Harte is defined as a cooperative group enterprise in which all must participate actively in order to benefit. This interdependence is stressed continually. Group solidarity is further increased by references to the hazards of the drinking society, due to its normative alcohol use and to its misunderstanding of and hostility toward alcoholics. By the end of approximately three weeks, the formerly isolated alcoholics feel and act like members of a mutually protective network. They return to Stockton with a desire to maintain these relationship bonds, which the operations of the program in Stockton are arranged to facilitate.

In Stockton, the program makes available other social settings that promote the continuing association of sober alcoholics with each other, so that they remain embedded in positive social networks. A steady schedule of group meetings and social activities is offered as is an opportunity to visit with former and present participants in the program, and with the staff. Meetings are seen as essential to the building of new social networks. They provide support and confirmation of the identity of each person in the program as an alcoholic and as a human being. The friendships and associations formed during participation in the program activities are seen as replacing those with former drinking buddies.

When a patient leaves Bret Harte to return to Stockton, he is always accompanied by another patient or a member of the staff, since this is recognized as a difficult moment. Furthermore, no one is discharged from Bret Harte after his initial period of residence without having an appropriate place to go.

Unlike the vast majority of programs for the alcoholic, this program does not see its responsibility as ending when the person has gone through the program. A basic tenet is the idea that whatever change takes place does not reside within the person, but includes every aspect of the patient's life, so the staff is especially concerned with the nature of the social context the person returns to when he leaves. If he returns to the daily orbit that characterized his life befor his Bret Harte experience, he will more than likely drink again, no matter how positive his sojourn or how strong his new intentions. If he returns to new territories his chances are much better.

Reterritorialization proceeds along two avenues: One involves relocating persons physically and helping them change their daily environments and adopt new patterns of social action. The other involves reshaping the symbolic meaning of the everyday landscape and altering the value of the responses from the environment to the alcoholic. These objectives form two aspects of the same process.

In our program the unit of intervention is changed from the individual to his relationships with others and to the construction of social contexts where the message *don't drink* prevails. These new social contexts facilitate changes in the individual's drinking behavior. Moreover, the drug option is replaced by the option of human interaction. The minimal social changes essential to maintenance of sobriety, which our program attempts to promote, include frequent association with sober alcoholics; nonsolitary living arrangements, preferably with other sober alcoholics; an occupation of some sort, either employment or leisure activities (helping in the rehabilitation of other alcoholics is especially desirable); and participation in an array of social activities while sober (many alcoholics have never attended a social function, made love, or related to coworkers and friends while sober).

These changes cannot be accomplished merely by exhorting the alcoholic to change. The treatment program itself must embody such changes by reconstructing the social living space of the alcoholic through the provision of new social and physical arrangements.

COMPONENTS OF THE PROGRAM

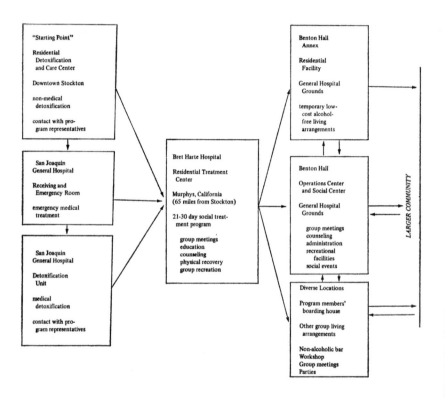

APPENDIX A

A POSTSCRIPT ON THIRTY WHO DIED

Note: Some of the persons selected in the sample for followup had died since participating in the program. Here are brief portraits* on thirty, a sad commentary on the often irreversible effects of alcoholism.

LUCILLE B.

Age 49. Grocery store checker. Came to Bret Harte already very ill. Transferred from Bret Harte to San Joaquin General Hospital, where she died.

Cause of Death: Hepatic coma, cirrhosis.

JAMES B.

Age 46. Had been working in nursery; very well liked there. Program lost contact with him. Appeared at Lodi Memorial Hospital asking to be brought back. Transferred to San Joaquin General Hospital, but was dead on arrival.

Cause of Death: Liver insufficiency, marked fatty cirrhosis.

DULCE B.

Age 58. Married, two grown children. Nurses' aide, but unemployed when she entered program. Started drinking immediately after leaving Bret Harte, only came to one meeting after that. Died seven months later.

Cause of Death: Liver failure, Laennec's cirrhosis, renal failure.

DONNA C.

Age 26. Married at time of admission. Also a barbiturate user. Very bright young girl, did very well at Bret Harte. Remained at Bret Harte for some time as volunteer worker for room and board. Then

---

* These notes were prepared by Aggie Shaw, chief counselor of the program.

returned to unhappy domestic situation in Stockton. Set fire to home while drunk, and died in the fire.

Cause of Death: Carbon monoxide poisoning during acute alcoholic intoxification.

RAY C.

Age 44. Farm laborer. Moved into Benton Hall after stay at Bret Harte, but continued to drink. Had six admissions to detoxification ward. Went to Bret Harte a second time, and remained sober for a period; everyone had high hopes for him. Then he left program, and two months later was stabbed to death in a park.

Cause of Death: Hemopericardium secondary to stab wound of heart.

ROY C.

Age 47. Married, with three grown children. Musician. Had been drinking all his life, and had never been in an alcoholism program before. Started drinking about a month after discharge from Bret Harte.

Cause of Death: Hepatic coma, portal cirrhosis.

"BUD" C.

Age 27. Separated from wife. Was employed as a printer, but lost job due to drinking. Severe diabetic. Drank even during his stay at Bret Harte.

Cause of Death: Diabetic coma, diabetes mellitus.

ROBERT C.

Age 53. Divorced. Unemployed cook. Had been in jail many times. Had attended a few A.A. meetings; had been in a state hospital for alcoholism treatment. After Bret Harte, he drank again briefly, then moved into the Annex and stayed sober for eight months. He then began missing doctor's appointments and meetings, and died ten months later.

Cause of Death: Hepatic coma.

JANET D.

Age 37. Had been a school teacher for fifteen years. At Bret Harte, she never appeared to comprehend the seriousness of her problem. Resumed drinking when she left Bret Harte, and died shortly thereafter.

Cause of Death: Hepatic coma due to cirrhosis of liver.

GEORGE E.

Age 63. Pensioner, lived alone in hotel. Had never been in an alcoholism program. Moved into Annex and participated in meetings for a short time, then moved back to hotel and resumed drinking. Died in hotel fire.

Cause of Death: Coronary artery insufficiency, arterio-sclerotic heart disease, bronchiopneumonia.

ROBERT F.

Age 49. Divorced. Dentist. Had gone to a few A.A. meetings; had never remained sober for any period of time. Stayed sober for a while after his stay at Bret Harte, but then had driver's license revoked and stopped attending meetings. Found dead at home by his son.

Cause of Death: Acute pulmonary edema.

BERNARD G.

Age 47. Never married, lived alone. Farm laborer all his life. Participated in program after stay at Bret Harte, but resumed drinking. Drank on and off until he died.

Cause of Death: Hepatic failure, probable cirrhosis.

HORTENCIA H.

Age 42. Divorced. Indian woman who had worked as a maid. Was living in a park at time of admission to Bret Harte. Left Bret Harte against advice, although she was still very sick and confused. Was hit and killed by a car while drunk.

Cause of Death: Extensive blunt trauma to the trunk and extremities.

JORGE H.

Age 31. Unmarried farm laborer. Moved here from Santa Domingo four years ago, began drinking at that time. Did very well after a long stay at Bret Harte, but then became involved with a woman alcoholic and began drinking again with her.

Cause of Death: Acute hepatic failure, chronic ethanolic cirrhosis.

WILLIS L.

Age 60. Married to 38 year old woman who was also an alcoholic. Had worked as a welder. Was very ill when admitted to Bret Harte. He considered moving into Annex, but returned to wife instead. He died a month later.

Cause of Death: Cardiorespiratory failure, cor pulmonale, pulmonary emphysema and fibrosis, arteriosclerotic heart disease.

CECIL M.

Age 52. Divorced. Had been a truck driver. While at Bret Harte, was very concerned about his health. Moved into Annex for a month, then left and resumed drinking. Five months later, after several admissions to detoxification ward, he died.

Cause of Death: Acute gastrointestinal bleeding, esophaegeal varices, Laennec's cirrhossis, chronic alcoholism, hepatic insufficiency.

DELMAR M.

Age 53. Divorced. Self-employed contractor. Had been given aversion treatment at Woodside Acres. Was admitted twice to Bret Harte, the second time leaving against advice. He was reported drunk immediately after leaving, and died five months later.

Cause of Death: Gastrointestinal hemorrhage, bleeding esophageal varices, fatty nutritional cirrhosis.

SIXTO M.

Age 41. Never married. Had worked as a gardener. Was very ill when admitted to Bret Harte and had to be transferred to San Joaquin General Hospital. Went home, and died shortly thereafter.

Cause of Death: Hepatic failure, Laennec's cirrhosis.

DONALD N.

Age 47. Never married. Worked as cook in a labor camp. After his stay at Breat Harte, he could not be talked out of returning to the labor camp. He resumed drinking, was admitted twice to detoxification ward, and then died.

Cause of Death: Acute pancreatitis, fatty metamorphosis of liver.

JACK O.

Age 61. Married. Board member of small corporation, formerly owner. Had been in many alcoholism treatment programs: Shaddel's in Seattle, Warm Springs, Woodside Acres, a few A.A. meetings. After stay at Bret Harte, was sober for a year, then stopped participating in program. Died in alcoholic seizure.

Cause of Death: Acute myocardial infarction due to arteriosclerotic coronary artery disease, diabetes mellitus.

WANDA O.

Age 48. Divorced, alienated from family because of her drinking. Very pretty woman. Also dependent on barbiturates. Died in San Joaquin General Hospital.

Cause of Death: Overdose of barbiturates and alcohol, lobar pneumonia, fatty nutritional cirrhosis.

MONA R.

Age 40. Separated from husband who also had drinking problem. Had worked as nurses' aide. Left Bret Harte against advice and was in jail shortly thereafter. Lost touch with her after her release from jail.

Cause of Death: Fatty nutritional cirrhosis of the liver.

ED S.

Age 38. Truck driver. Had been drinking since adolescence. After stay at Bret Harte, was sober for eight months and had driver's license reinstated. Then became involved with woman alcoholic and resumed drinking, lost driver's license. Jumped off Oakland Bay Bridge.

Cause of Death: Suicidal drowning.

APPENDIX B

COMPONENTS OF AN
ALCOHOLIC REHABILITATION PROGRAM

1. *Physical Arrangements*

Unit A: Residential Treatment Center

Size: Live-in units capable of housing up to fifty persons, larger units are not desirable. Units in design and character should resemble a a home more than a hospital. They should include the following features.

a. *Sleeping areas*: Several small dormitory-like areas sleeping six to ten persons are preferable to large or smaller areas.

b. *Day room*: A multiple-purpose area for everyday activities, large enough to accommodate all patients at one time for meetings, group discussions, and lectures, this room can, at other times, be used as a recreational area for games, parties, and such.

c. *Nursing area*: Treatment facilities and supplies for emergency care, should be centrally located. The traditional glassed-in nurse's station is *not* desirable; arrangements should encourage nursing personnel to occupy the day room when not engaged in technical duties. (Isolated office space for all professional personnel should be kept to a minimum.)

d. *Community kitchen*: This should be equipped with coffee urn and facilities and utensils to permit food preparation and eating twenty-four hours a day. This may or may not be combined with:

e. *Kitchen and dining area*: Make this large enough to prepare and serve meals to all residents. (Administrative rules should be relaxed as far as possible to allow patients to participate in the preparation and serving of meals.)

Location: It is desirable that this unit be some distance away from the area from which the alcoholic population is drawn. A rural setting is particularly desirable in that it enhances the retreat atmosphere of this stage of treatment and also in that it makes alcohol more remote.

Unit B: Operations and Social Center

Size: This should be one large unit with some housing accommodations for at least 20 to 30 persons. It is best that the features of this unit be more homelike than institutional, although this is not so important for Unit B as it is for Unit A. Unit B should include the following areas:

a. *Housing accommodations*: These should consist of one to four-person rooms, for occupancy by individuals leaving Unit A for whom suitable living arrangements in the community have not yet been made.

b. *Community kitchen and dining area*: Arrange this in such a way as to permit group meal preparation and dining for the unit's occupants and so that it is accessible twenty-four hours a day.

c. *Meeting room*: A multiple purpose area large enough to accommodate large groups of people for meetings and for recreational activities such as potluck dinners, parties, and dances, this area could also serve as a lounge for the unit occupants. (A nearby community hall might also serve this purpose if a large enough building cannot be obtained.)

d. *Offices*: This unit should contain offices for the program administration, one or more physicians, a social worker, and one or more counselors. Offices should be clustered about a lounge/waiting room area. This entire arrangement may be very simple, and in fact care should be taken that it not be more elaborately equipped than the rest of the unit.

Location: It is preferable that this unit be located near an inner city area, close to public transportation and close to temporary work opportunities. It should be easily accessible to the majority of the program participants, who will reside outside the unit.

Subsidiary Units: Other units are not essential to the program but are desirable when and if resources become available:

a. *Workshop*: It is desirable to provide the opportunity for some sort of occupation that is productive and, if possible, financially profitable. A crafts workshop, a gas station, a store, an unskilled labor contracting firm are among the possibilities.

b. *Additional housing*: Housing in more than one locality, especially if such housing contains an area which can be used for meetings and informal get-togethers, is also desirable. A boarding house, a small hotel, or an apartment house represent desirable expansions of the basic program.

c. *Bar/restaurant*: A centrally located bar/restaurant could provide a comfortable area in which to spend free time. (Of course, the bar would be nonalcoholic.) Such an establishment would be patronized regularly by program participants and could also provide a paid job. For the alcoholic on the street, it would offer an alternative environment.

2. *Personnel of the Program*

Professional staff within the program should be kept to a minimum; as many positions as possible, perhaps including professional positions, should be filled by individuals who have had unfortunate experiences with alcohol and who participate in the activities of the program.

a. *Physician*: At least one physician should be on call at all times to handle emergencies in Unit A, where patients are going through the severe stages of withdrawal. A physician is also needed to examine patients about to be admitted to Unit A and to make regular rounds in Unit A, and for office hours in Unit B for the continued care of all who require it.

b. *Nurses*: Nurses should be on duty full time in Unit A; they should be chosen on the basis of both nursing skill and ability to relate positively and comfortably to an alcoholic client.

c. *Social Worker*: At least one social worker is useful to help program members deal with public agencies, obtain financial aid, and develop employment opportunities.

d. *Counselors*: These members of the treatment team are most directly involved in personal contact with patients: they recruit new patients from the general hospital and from alcoholic hangouts, they lead group meetings, and they counsel individual patients more or less formally.

The counselors should be sober alcoholics, themselves. Initially they may be recruited from Alcoholics Anonymous and similar groups. Once the program is in operation, counselors will largely be drawn from the ranks of the participants.

The housekeeping work on both units, less complex administrative tasks, and whatever other routine work is required should be performed by the clients, especially those residing in the units. The more work, responsibility, and prestige distributed throughout the community of participants, the more effective the program will be.

3. *Program Activities*

All activities serve the primary purpose of bringing program participants together, strengthening relationships, reinforcing social support for sobriety, and occupying time in a constructive fashion. The most important activities are:

a. *Group meetings*: These should be held about twice daily for all residents in Unit A and at least once daily in Unit B and/or in other easily accessible locations in the city. All participants should be strongly encouraged to attend group meetings regularly, and member's prolonged absence from them should be noticed and inquired into.

At these meetings, personal experiences with alcohol and with sobriety will be exchanged and the philosophy of the program will be explained and explored. There are no constraints on the kinds of problems that may be raised and discussed. The leader will encourage (but not force) all present to participate.

Arrangements should allow for informal conversation after the close of the meeting.

b. *Recreation*: Potluck dinners, parties, bingo games, dances, and so forth, will be held regularly in Unit B. At least one evening per week some such informal activity should be arranged. Picnics, group excursions and other entertainments are also desirable.

c. *Work projects*: Occasionally, when the opportunity arises, it is desirable for as many participants as possible to engage in work projects; these could include spring cleaning and making improvements in the program facilities or helping a program member get a new house into livable condition.

Smaller groups of members might provide services to the program (such as a newsletter) or to the community at large on a more regular basis.

4. *Administrative Arrangements*

Since new participants are drawn from their repetitive course through skid row, hospital, and jail, it is necessary to make arrangements with hospital emergency and detoxification services and with the judicial system, if possible, to permit counselors to make regular visits to such facilities for recruiting purposes.

Arrangements should be made with funding sources, city, county, and state, to permit the employment by the program of sober alcoholics, who are uniquely suited for such work but who may have criminal records.

Permission also has to be obtained from responsible officials to permit participants, especially residents of Unit A, to perform food preparation and other such services, sometimes restricted by law.

APPENDIX C

COMPONENTS OF A RESIDENTIAL
DETOXIFICATION AND CARE PROGRAM

1. *Physical Arrangements*

The residential detoxification center is a locality capable of housing fifteen to twenty-five persons. In character it resembles a home more than a hospital or institution. The center includes the following features:

a. *Sleeping area*: one large room with fifteen beds which allows for observation by residential staff.

b. *Living room*: a comfortably furnished area for everyday activities and informal interaction among the residents.

c. *Community kitchen*: equipped with coffee urn and other utensils and facilities to permit food preparation twenty-four hours a day. Basic meals are provided by outside sources.

d. *Dining area*: large enough to permit all residents to eat meals together. Residents participate in preparation, serving, and clean-up.

e. *Staff office area*: A small office area available for intake and for staff record keeping.

f. *Bathing facilities*: sufficient to serve the needs of the residents.

g. *Storage area*: for clothes and personal effects of residents.

2. *Location*

Within the inner city, to allow ready access for the majority of the alcoholic population.

3. *Personnel*

Professional staffing of the center is kept at a minimum; most positions are filled by sober alcoholics.

a. *Medical Staffing*: available on call and from general hospital.

b. *Program Supervisor*: he is responsible for direct supervision of the activities of the center and serves as a coordinator between this unit and agencies within the community.

c. *Residential attendants*: five residential attendants, all recovered alcoholics, are assigned eight-hour shifts to provide twenty-four hour, seven days a week coverage of the center. They are responsible for admitting and providing care to the clients during their stay at the center. They also direct the activities of volunteers.

d. *Volunteers*: Two or more volunteers work on each eight hour shift; many of these are recovered alcoholics who are participating in local programs. They assist the residential attendants in providing care for the clients and in engaging in interaction with them.

e. *Housekeeper*: one housekeeper is assigned to the unit to be responsible for overall housekeeping and janitorial duties. (Clients also assist in upkeep of their area and the unit.)

Daily involvement by groups and agencies concerned with the alcoholic such as Alcoholics Anonymous, alcoholic rehabilitation clinics, and other agencies offering services to the alcoholic.

4. *Activities*

All activities at the center serve the primary purpose of establishing and strengthening personal relationships among the clients and between the clients and representatives of those agencies that seek to assist them with their alcohol problems. Within a context of acceptance and understanding, clients are encouraged (but not coerced) to take advantage of the resources available to them in the community. All activities within the center are undertaken in a personal and individualized manner.

a. *Admission*: clients are received as self-referrals and from hospital emergency rooms after medical evaluation, from law-enforcement agencies, mental-health clinics, Alcoholics Anonymous, social welfare agencies, alcoholic rehabilitation clinics, county alcoholism treatment programs, Salvation Army, church organizations, and other agencies.

Upon arrival at the center, the client is greeted by an attendant or volunteer, who shows him his bed, allows him to bathe and shave, provides clothing if needed, and brings the client to the living room of the center for coffee and food, introducing him to other residents.

b. *Evaluation*: evaluation of each client's situation is carried out by the attendant on an informal basis during the course of the client's stay at the center. It is felt that more reliable intake information may be obtained gradually than at one time. (In the event of suspected medical complications, the client is taken to a general hospital for evaluation; he may be returned to the center following this examination if the medical problem can be managed on an outpatient basis. Hospitalization in the detoxification unit is available if indicated.)

c. *Interaction among residents*: all residents are encouraged to interact among themselves, informally discussing their problems and experiences with alcohol and other life problems and their plans for the future.

d. *Interaction with agency representatives*: representatives of community agencies offering services to alcoholics visit the center frequently to meet with the residents and explain their services.

e. *Referral system*: as each client's needs are ascertained, referrals are made by the center staff to the appropriate agency. Whenever possible, arrangements are made for the client to meet with a representative of this agency while he is still in residence.

f. *Formal meetings in the community*: although the activities within the center are informal, each client is encouraged to attend formal meetings of such groups as Alcoholics Anonymous and the county alcoholism treatment program, while still in residence at the center. It is felt to be advantageous for the client to establish initial contact with such groups in the community as a starting point for recovery.

5. *Administrative Arrangements*

Since the clients of the residential detoxification center are drawn from a repetitive course through skid row, hospital, and jail, arrangements are made with law enforcement agencies, hospital emergency services, social service agencies, and all other agencies which may make initial contact with alcoholics, to refer alcoholics in need of detoxification to the center.

APPENDIX D

A PARADIGM FOR THE ANALYSIS OF
ALCOHOLISM TREATMENT PROGRAMS

As an initial step in the direction of codifying the analysis of alcoholism treatment programs, we here set forth a paradigm of the concepts and questions central to our approach. The components of this paradigm have emerged in the foregoing pages as we critically examined the vocabularies, postulates, and conceptions now current in the field and analyzed one program in depth. The paradigm will serve to guide inquiry and organize observation in the future, so that new and existing programs can be comprehensively described and compared.

Frame

Within any treatment program, all of the components that can be abstracted for description constitute an organized system. Decisions made about any one element interact with and constrain decisions about other elements within the larger structure. For the sake of clarity and systematic analysis, however, each component is here introduced and described individually.

Intra - System

1. Definition of Alcoholism

Within every program explicit or implicit definitions exist.

Terminological Universe: In what set of terms is an individual defined as alcoholic? Physiological? Psychological? Social? What combination and emphasis?

Consensus: Discrepancies in definition among staff? Between staff and clients? If differences exist do they change over time or remain stable? (e.g., with increasing time-in-treatment, do patients' definitions begin to converge with staff definitions?)

Criteria of Diagnosis: What "diagnostic signs" are relevant? (e.g., physical exam, lab tests, social history).

Criteria of Admission: Are criteria other than those defining alcoholism used in deciding whether to admit an individual to a program? How are they justified?

[77]

2. Institutional Location

Institutional setting and physical location have direct consequences for the choice of treatment; in a general hospital the alcoholic will likely be administered drugs, in a mental health clinic he is likely to be labelled and treated psychiatrically, etc.

Setting: Hospital ward? Private psychiatric hospital? Community mental health clinic? Residential program? What constraints or treatment are imposed by the institutional setting?

Affiliations: Hospital? Judicial system? Public health department? Teaching or research facility?

Physical location: Metropolitan area? Small community? Country retreat? One location or several?

3. Unit of Treatment

Every program delimits the forms of intervention or treatment.

Who or what: Who is being treated? If it is the person, then what is the target—a part of the physical organism? A psychological conflict? The *whole* (*individual*) person? Is the unit a social system such as the family or segments of the community or of the society at large? Is the target system the alcoholic's *life space* (i.e., the person embedded in a patterned setting); is it the space *between,* or *something within*?

Source and target: Is the avowed source of the problem also the target for treatment or intervention? e.g., if alcoholism is seen as a problem of living, how extensive is involvement in the person's life?

4. Time Span of Treatment

Every program contains definitions of the duration of treatment required. Every program maintains contact with its clientele for specific lengths of time, varying from a limited intervention to a life-time of association.

Treatment status: How long does treatment last? Is it confined to periods of physical illness? Psychological or social crisis? Duration of in-patient status in hospital? Is there a specific end point to treatment? If so, is it based on some criteria of *cure* or is it an arbitrarily chosen length of time and commitment of the program's resources? When is it terminated?

Follow-up: Does a program monitor the status of their discharged clients at some point after treatment? Is there a minimal containing involvement or simply a periodic check, if there is any follow-up at all?

Continued Association: Are there stages and phases of treatment or association with the program? (e.g., a period of intensive treatment followed by a series of group meetings?) Is treatment ever com-

pleted or is it seen as going on for life? Are there stages of involvement with professional personnel? (e.g., treatment may be lifelong
with little expense; recovered alcoholics can maintain each other's
sobriety and well-being without professional help after initial phases.)

5. *Rationale for Treatment*

Every program has an explicit and/or implicit rationale for its existence
and its activities.

Avowed Purpose: What is considered the primary purpose of the
treatment program? Reversal or amelioration of the condition? Reduction of psychological pain?   Reduction of socially undesirable behavior such as crime? Reduction of society's economic costs (to
welfare system, health care system, judicial system?) Changes in everyday living? Creation of supportive social system?

Consensus: How much agreement is there among staff and between
staff and patients regarding the rationale for treatment?

Mystification: How congruent or discrepant are the program's avowed
goals with its actual operations? Whose purposes are served by the
discrepancies?

6. *Unit of Intervening Agent*

Programs vary according to what is utilized as the principal intervening
agent.

Change agent: Is it a technological tool (e.g., tranquilizing and sedating drugs, chemical alcohol antagonists, aversive conditioning techniques?) An individual physician or mental health professional? A
system in one setting (e.g., a therapeutic community in a hospital);
a system extending into different settings, both at one point in time
and over time?

Role of patient: Are patients seen as passive recipients of treatment,
or are they actively involved in the treatment process?

7. *Treatment Modalities*

Treatment strategies utilize different modalities, ranging from a single
technological instrument to a complex social organization.

Which modality: What is the primary modality of treatment; chemical,
psychotherapy, behavior modification techniques, education, social involvement? What is the rationale for the use of this mode in contrast to some
others?

Balance and integration: If more than one modality is utilized, what is the
balance among them? How are they integrated (e.g., separate and distinct
inputs, or aspects of a large process of change)?

8. *Orientation toward Psychoactive Drugs*

Programs define and use drugs in fundamentally different ways.

Framework: Are legal and illegal drugs, alcohol and "medications" defined within a single framework? Are differential assets and liabilities attached to different drugs? What educational inputs are patients given about the nature of psychoactive drug action (including alcohol).

Therapy: Are drugs used as part of treatment? Under what conditions? Are alcoholics encouraged to substitute prescribed drugs for alcohol on a maintenance basis? Are they permitted to do this though it may not be a formal part of treatment? Are other drugs seen as functionally equivalent to alcohol and therefore discouraged?

9. *Model of Recovery*

The issue of recovery in part determines criteria for both the success of the treatment and the time when patient and program should be separated from one another.

Success and failure: What are the criteria of success and failure? Is it believed that successfully treated alcoholics cannot or can *drink socially*? Is cessation of drinking the most important or sole criterion? What behaviors on the part of their clientele will program staff be satisfied with?

Recovery: What constitutes recovery? Are social changes (employment, new leisure activities, new housing arrangements) seen as part of recovery?

Sobriety: What are seen as the basic requirements of continued sobriety? Self understanding? Successful completion of the program? Changes in membership within social networks? Participation in new social landscapes? Continuous reinforcement and social support?

10. *Attribution of Credit*

Credit for change is distributed differently among programs.

Who or what: In particular instances of "success" or "failure" who or what is credited or blamed? Are "successes" due to the program and "failures" due to individual alcoholics?

Dropouts: On what basis are people dropped from the program? Do failures get psychiatric labels? What efforts are made to recover and continue work with the "fallen?"

EXTRA - SYSTEM

1. *Generation of New Social Forms*

Programs either leave the basic arrangements surrounding the patient unaltered or they invent new forms which in turn intersect with the larger socialstructure.

New Arrangements: What new social arrangements are evolved for the "treatment" of the alcoholic? How do these alter the balance of the lives of their membership compared to life before involvement in the program? What relationships do these new groups carry on with the larger community at what level? (e.g. an economic or political force, an alternative structure for meeting basic economic and social needs). How is life in the surrounding community different as a result of the development of a new subcommunity out of the program?

2. Large Scale Consequences

The model of treatment for the alcoholic employed has consequences both short and long term for the community's understanding and approach to the problem.

Treatment Consequences: Is the model implicit a replication of existing forms and thereby a confirmation that alcoholism has and is being treated appropriately? Is there a new form of treatment involved that is likely to affect the development of future programs? Does a new treatment form carry with it an alteration of the conception of alcoholism itself?

Social Consequences: What large scale and long range implications for the conception and treatment of alcoholism are generated by a model of treatment?

3. Moral Implications

Every form of treatment generates questions about the moral dimensions implicit in the method.

Values: What priorities are stressed by the boundaries of treatment (e.g. concern with "civil rights" versus submission to "treatment;" the allocation of time and resources, etc.) What message is implicit in the treatment process that communicates how people should be treated in the larger sense? Are some models more or less "dehumanizing?" (e.g. social treatment or aversive therapy).

Images: What messages are communicated to the alcoholic about himself through participation in the treatment program? What image of the alcoholic is presented to the larger community?

APPENDIX E

ADMINISTRATIVE PROBLEMS
IN THE DEVELOPMENT OF A PROGRAM

Most agencies and staffs who have worked with alcoholics in the past have had unrewarding experiences. Members of nursing staffs at hospitals have seen the frequent return of many patients, and some have never witnessed recovery. Physicians working in emergency rooms and attending the medical floors have had similar experiences. Our first approach at San Joaquin General Hospital was to hold staff orientation seminars; we realized that merely telling the staff that alcoholism could be treated successfully was not sufficient. We exposed them to recovered alcoholics who were employed as counselors on the program. Interacting with these persons has had considerable impact on the hospital personnel, as many had never met alcoholics with years of continuous sobriety. When the counselors described their drinking careers and related their own repeated experiences in emergency rooms, the staff began to exhibit some changes in attitude.

We had to overcome the built-in prejudices that many persons feel toward the alcoholic. Many persons have experienced alcoholism in their own families and have strong feelings about drinking. Prejudice about the alcoholic is perhaps best overcome through the demonstration of sobriety by the recovered alcoholic. During the first few months of the program we encouraged recovered alcoholic patients who had remained sober and who had reconstructed their lives to return to the general hospital to visit with the nursing and professional staff. Many clients were very willing to do this and would drop in, even just to say "thank you for taking care of me while I was so ill" and to give progress reports on what had happened to them since hospitalization. This technique was not only dramatic to many of the staff members but was helpful to the patients as well.

The remoteness of the residential treatment unit at Bret Harte Hospital, sixty-five miles from Stockton, presented special problems. The nursing staff at this hospital had been oriented toward chronic care and programmed for long-term hospitalization and care. When the alcoholism program was outlined to them, many fears and anxieties became very obvious. A first organizational response was to increase the staff and require a male attendant to be on duty at all times ostensibly to help protect the nurses. Since the nurses had had little or no experience in caring for the alcoholic patients, they had no understanding of the behavior of the alcoholic in a treatment program. There have been significant changes of attitude at this treatment unit. Staff and patients have become friends. For example, three nurses have married patients to date.

The patients have demonstrated to the staff that they are neither dangerous nor difficult, once alcohol is removed from their lives. There are frequent reunions and get-togethers at the treatment unit, to which the patients return at monthly intervals, a fact that again serves to remind the staff that recovery is possible. Many of the patients have expressed their appreciation and gratitude for what the staff did for them. This expression of gratitude has strengthened the commitment and involvement of the staff, which is so necessary for a successful program.

Another step taken before the beginning of the alcoholism program was to discuss our social treatment approach with the various county agencies involved, such as law enforcement, welfare, and the Department of Motor Vehicles. Again, most of these agencies were somewhat prejudiced as a result of past experience with alcoholics. Nonetheless, their cooperation has been very satisfactory. Most agencies agreed immediately to cooperate with the new approach. Without exception, they have held to this commitment and have been most helpful in the development of this program. Many agreed that the traditional approaches were not successful and so were willing to go along with an alternative treatment approach.

APPENDIX F

Instruments Used in the Study:

FOLLOW - UP QUESTIONNAIRE

_____

(Date)

NAME OF RESPONDENT_____

NAME OF INTERVIEWER_____

I. I am Mr./Miss_____. I am working for the San Francisco Medical Center and we are talking to people who have gone through San Joaquin General Hospital with an alcohol problem. I would appreciate it very much if you could spend 15 minutes with me.

II. Have you been treated at the General Hospital? Yes_____ No_____
If yes, then ask about the last time.
The last time you were treated at the General Hospital what happened? Where were you sent?
(Ask for whether they went to Bret Harte, a General Hospital ward, or were discharged, etc.)

III. We'd like to talk to you about where you are living now. (Be specific)
What sort of place is it? (hotel, boarding house, private home, etc.)
With whom are you living now? (family, friends, alone)
How many people, what relationships, etc.

IV. Were you living at the same place before you went to San Joaquin General Hospital or Bret Harte?
If yes, check here _____
If no, what sort of place was it?_____
With whom were you living there?

V. Are you doing any work now?   Do you have a job?
If yes, then ask if it is full- or part-time.
If no, then ask if they do any unpaid work and what.

VI. If working, how do you spend your spare time? If not working, how do you spend your days? (If activities listed, ask if done alone or, if with others, with whom?)

[84]

VII. Were you doing any work before you went to the hospital?

Did you have a job? If yes, then ask if full or part time.

If no, then ask if they did any unpaid work and what.

VIII. If you were working, how did you spend your spare time?

If you were not working, how did you spend your days? (If activities listed, ask if done alone, and, if with others, whom?)

IX. Now let's talk about your experience at Bret Harte. When did you first hear about Project Faith and from whom?

How did you happen to get to Bret Harte? (Probe for whether it was their choice or were they talked into it).

X. How did you feel up there? Comfortable?   Uncomfortable?
What do you think of the different parts of the program?

LECTURES: _____
COUNSELORS: _____
NURSES: _____
DOCTORS: _____
BEING WITH OTHERS WITH THE SAME
    PROBLEM: _____
BEING AWAY FROM YOUR USUAL
    LOCATION: _____
THE MINISTER AND RELIGION: _____

XI. Of all parts of the program, which is the most important and which is the least important. (See list in number 10. *Show card* to person).

XII. If you were planning the program, how would you make it better? What would you add?

XIII. Many of the patients from Project Faith still go to meetings. How about you? Do you go to any meetings? If yes, which meetings do you go to? (Show card).

BENTON HALL_____X PER MONTH
A.A._____X PER MONTH (which AA group?)
A.R.C._____X PER MONTH
IRIS'S HOUSE_____X PER MONTH

XIV. Do you visit Benton Hall? How many times were you there last month?

What activities did you go to?

XV. Did you make any new friends through Project Faith?

Which ones do you still see often?

XVI. Are you drinking now? If yes, How Much?

Were you drunk since you left Project Faith?

XVII. Are you taking any medication now to help you stay sober?

If yes, what type pills do you take? (show card and numbered pills)

PILLS:

WHICH ONES?	HOW OFTEN?
1.	
2.	
3.	
4.	
5.	

BIOGRAPHICAL NOTES

ROBERT G. O'BRIANT is Medical Director of San Joaquin County Addictive Services in Stockton, California where he has directed comprehensive programs for the treatment of alcoholism and drug addiction, including detoxification wards, residential treatment centers and extensive social involvement programs. He received an award in 1971 from the California State Mental Health Association for outstanding program development in the field of alcoholism. Dr. O'Briant has formerly served as Medical Director of San Joaquin General Hospital. He is a member of the American Academy of Medical Administrators and is consultant to the Alcoholism Program for San Francisco City and County, to the University of California at Santa Cruz in their Alcoholism Program for Indian Counselors, and to the San Joaquin County Medical Society. Dr. O'Briant received his M. D. from Marquette University in 1963.

HENRY L. LENNARD is Professor of Medical Sociology in the Department of Psychiatry at the San Francisco Campus of the University of California, where he directs the Family Study Station and the Laboratory for the Study of Psychoactive Drugs and Social Behavior. Previously, Dr. Lennard was codirector of the Mental Health Training and Research Program in the Department of Sociology and the Bureau of Applied Social Research at Columbia University, and also served on the Graduate Faculties of the New School and the University of Colorado. He has been consultant to the Departments of Psychiatry of the Downstate Medical Center, State University of New York and of Roosevelt Hospital. Dr. Lennard received his Ph.D. degree from Columbia in 1955. He is author of THE ANATOMY OF PSYCHOTHERAPY; PATTERNS IN HUMAN INTERACTION: An Introduction to Clinical Sociology; and MYSTIFICATION AND DRUG MISUSE.

STEVEN D. ALLEN is a lecturer in Ambulatory and Community Medicine at the San Francisco campus of the University of California and a Research Associate at the Laboratory for the Study of Psychoactive Drugs and Social Behavior. He has previously worked as a clinical psychologist in the San Francisco Community Mental Health Services and in the Adolescent Drug Abuse Treatment Program at Mendocino State Hospital, Talmage, California. He has also participated in program evaluation of several drug abuse treatment programs. Allen received his Ph.D. in psychology from the University of California at Berkeley in 1972. He is a contributor to MYSTIFICATION AND DRUG MISUSE.

DONALD C. RANSOM is assistant professor of Ambulatory and Community Medicine at the San Francisco Campus of the University of California, where he is active in the development of family medicine. Dr. Ransom is also on the staff of Family Study Station, the Laboratory for the Study of Psychoactive Drugs and Social Behavior, and the Sex Advisory and Counseling Unit at the San Francisco Medical Center. Ransom received an A.B. in social relations from Harvard (1965), an M.A. in sociology (1966), and a Ph.D. in clinical psychology (1970), both from the University of California at Berkeley. He is coauthor with Dr. Lennard of MYSTIFICATION AND DRUG MISUSE.

SELECTED BIBLIOGRAPHY

Alcoholics Anonymous: The Story of How Many Thousands of Men and Women Have Recovered from Alcoholism, 2nd ed. New York, Alcoholics Anonymous Publishing, 1955.

Aspects of Alcoholism, vol. 1. Philadelphia, Lippincott, 1963.

Aspects of Alcoholism, vol. w. Philadelphia, Lippincott, 1966.

Bacon, S. D.: Drug abuse and alcohol abuse: the social problem perspective. *Prosecutor* (Chicago), 5:32-36, 1969.

Bales, R. F.: Social therapy for a social disorder: compulsive drinking. *J Soc Issues, 1*:14-22, 1945.

Bateson, G.: Toward a theory of alcoholism: the cybernetics of "self". Contribution No. 60, Hawaii, Oceanic Institute.

Beard, J. D., and Knott, D. H. Fluid and electrolyte balance during acute withdrawal in chronic alcoholic patients. *JAMA, 204*: 135, April, 1968.

Blum, E. M., and Blum, R. H.: *Alcoholism*. San Francisco, Jossey-Bass, 1967.

Cahalan, D.: *Problem Drinkers*. San Francisco, Jossey-Bass, 1970.

Cantanzaro, R. J.; *Alcoholism: The Total Treatment Approach*. Springfield, Thomas, 1968.

Chafetz, M. E., Blane, H. T., and Hill M. J.: *Frontiers of Alcoholism*. New York, Science House, 1970.

Chafetz, M. E., and Demone, H. W.: *Alcoholism and Society*. New York, Oxford University Press, 1962.

Davies, D. L: Stabilized addiction and normal drinking in recovered alcohol addicts. In H. Steinberg (Ed.), *Scientific Basis of Drug Dependence*. London, J. & A. Churchill Ltd., 1969.

Dunn, J. H., and Clay, M. L.: Physicians look at a general hospital alcoholism service. *Q J Stud Alcohol, 32*: 162-167, 1971.

Fox, R.: The perils of controlled drinking. In C. D. Smithers (Ed.) *Understanding Alcoholism: For the Patient, the Family, and the Employer*. New York, Charles Scribner's Sons, 71, 1968.

Gardner-Thorpe, and Benjamin S.: Peripheral neuropathy after disulfiram administration. *J Neurol Neurosurg Psychiat, 34*: 253-259, 1971.

Hill, M. J., and Bland, H. T.: Evaluation of psychotherapy with alcoholics: a critical review. *Q J Stud Alcohol 28*: 76-204, 1967.

Jellinek, E. M.: *The Disease Concept of Alcoholism*. New Haven, Hillhouse, 1960.

Lennard, H. L., Epstein, L. J., Bernstein, A., and Ransom, D. C.: Hazards implicit in prescribing psychoactive drugs. *Science, 169*: 438-441, 1970.

Lennard, H. L., and Bernstein, A.: *Patterns in Human Interaction.* San Francisco, Jossey-Bass, 1969.

Lolli, G., Serianni, E., Golder, G. M., and Fegiz, P.: *Alcohol in Italian Culture.* Glencoe, The Free Press, 1958.

Maddox, G. L., and McCall, B. C.: Drinking among teen-agers: a sociological interpretation of alcohol use. *Q J Stud Alcohol,* June 24, 1971.

Mendelson, J. H., and Mello, N. K.: A disease as an organizer for biochemical research. In A. J. Mandell and M. P. Mandell, (Eds.), *Psychochemical Research in Man.* New York, Academic Press, 1969.

Mendelson, J. H., Mello, N. K., and Solomon, P.: Small group drinking behavior: an experimental study of chronic alcoholics. In Association for Research in Nervous and Mengal Disease. *The Addictive States,* vol. 46. Baltimore, The William Wilkins Co., 1968.

Moody, P. M.: Attitudes of nursing and nursing students toward alcoholism treatment. *Q J Stud Alcohol, 32:* 172-175, 1971.

Pittman, D. J., and Gordon, C. W.: *Revolving Door: A study of the Chronic Police Case Inebriate.* Glencoe, The Free Press, 1958.

Pittman, D. J., and Snyder, D. R. (Eds.): Society and Drinking Patterns. New York, Wiley, 1962.

Plaut, T. F. A.: *Alcohol Problems: A Report to the Nation by the Cooperative Commission on the Study of Alcoholism.* New York, Oxford University Press, 1967.

Popham, R. E., and Schmidt, W.: *A Decade of Alcoholic Research.* Toronto, University of Toronto Press, 1962.

Rubington, E.: The nature of social problems. *Br J Addict, 64:* 31-46, 1969.

Sadoun, R., Lolli, G., and Silverman, M.: *Drinking in French Culture.* New Brunswick, N. J., Rutgers Center of Alcohol Studies, 1965.

Siegler, M., Osmond, H., and Newell, S.: Models of alcoholism. *Q J Stud Alcohol, 29:* 571-591, 1969.

Singer, E., Blane, H. T., and Kasschau, R.: Alcoholism and social isolation. *J Abnorm Soc Psychol, 69:* 681-685, 1964.

Snyder, C. R.: *Alcohol and the Jews: A Cultural Study of Drinking and Sobriety.* Glencoe, The Free Press, 1958.

Steinglass, P., Weiner, S., and Mendelson, J. H.: *Interactional Issues as Determinants of Alcoholism.* Mimeographed. Washington, D. C., National Institute of Mental Health, 1970.

Trice, H. M., and Roman, P. M.: Delabeling, relabeling, and Alcoholics Anonymous. *Social Problems, 17:* 538-546, 1970.

Ward, R. F., and Faillace, L. A.: The alcoholic and his helpers: a system view. *Quart J Stud Alcohol, 31:* 684-691, 1970.

Whitney, E. D. (Ed.): *World Dialogue on Alcohol and Drug Dependence.* Boston, Beacon Press, 1971.

Wilkinson, R.: *The Prevention of Drinking Problems: Alcohol Control and Cultural Influences.* New York, Oxford University Press, 1970.

INDEX